D1032202

Myth and Literature

CONCEPTS OF LITERATURE

GENERAL EDITOR: WILLIAM RIGHTER
Department of English
University of Warwick

Volumes in this series include

COMPARATIVE LITERATURE
Henry Gifford, *University of Bristol*

STYLE AND STYLISTICS
Graham Hough, *University of Cambridge*

LITERATURE AND DRAMA
Stanley Wells, *University of Birmingham*

ON REALISM
J. P. Stern, *University College, London*

THE TRANSFORMATIONS OF ALLEGORY
Gay Clifford, *University of Warwick*

Myth and Literature

William Righter

**Department of English,
University of Warwick**

ROUTLEDGE & KEGAN PAUL
LONDON AND BOSTON

WILLIAM WOODS COLLEGE LIBRARY

First published in 1975
by Routledge & Kegan Paul Ltd
Broadway House, 68–74 Carter Lane,
London EC4V 5EL and
9 Park Street
Boston, Mass. 02108, USA
Set in Linotype Pilgrim
and printed in Great Britain by
Cox & Wyman Ltd,
London, Fakenham and Reading
© William Righter 1975
No part of this book may be reproduced in
any form without permission from the
publisher, except for the quotation of brief
passages in criticism

ISBN 0 7100 8137 5

PN
56
M94
R5

Preface

A vast subject – and a short book in which to deal with the imaginative impact of one of the great cant words of our time. Yet behind the facile evocations some powerful necessities have given life to the concept of myth – and the very circumstances which have given life have served to create multiple demands which a single notion, clearly conceived, could hardly fulfil. I have examined this paradox in looking at the uses made of 'myth' in the modern literary imagination, both by writers for whom it represented a furthering of their own creative powers, or by critics for whom it represented an interpretative key. And finally I have tried to suggest those affinities by which the literary mind has claimed the powers of its touchstone, and sought through its re-invention of myth its own imagining and sense-making powers. A self-annihilating dream? Rather the conjunction of impasse and necessity which begins in open possibility and ends in diminishing returns. For all these uses of myth present a transformation from immediacy of demand into the plasticity of a conceptual device, growing steadily more pervasive because less distinct.

Although I do not mean to suggest a clear-cut historical development through the multiple senses of myth, the two epigraphs suggest in capsule form the poles of an historical transition, or at least a shift of sensibility from the hunger for myth to the saturation with myth. Of course the word itself has undergone a gradual transformation, a mixture of complication and dilution. One effect of this, in a world which accepts the vaguely mythicized elements of its everyday life, is the levelling of distinctions, such as Nietzsche's, between 'myth' and 'fiction'. For our own sensibility such blurrings are a happy form of intellectual accommodation. Auden has said, 'men have always lounged in myths', but perhaps in no time like the present.

Contents

Man today, stripped of myth, stands famished among all his pasts and must dig frantically for roots, be it among the most remote antiquities. What does our great historical hunger signify, our clutching about us of countless other cultures, our consuming desire for knowledge, if not the loss of myth, of a mythic home, the mythic womb?

Nietzsche 1872

In any case, at this very moment, the society in which I live is a society of myths. All of the elements which surround me are mythological elements.

Robbe-Grillet 1972

1

The consciousness of myth

1 *Stavrogin's dream*

Towards the end of the terrible confession which
Dostoevsky originally intended for *The Possessed* his
protagonist, Nicolai Stavrogin, describes 'the most unexpected dream' :

> I have never known the like of it. In the art gallery in
> Dresden there is a picture by Claude Lorraine. In the
> catalogue it is given as 'Acis and Galatea', but I have
> always called it, although I do not know why, 'The Golden
> Age'.... It was this picture I dreamt of, but not as a
> picture, but as if it were real life. The scene is set in a
> corner of the Greek Archipelago; blue caressing waves,
> islands and rocks, verdant shores, a magical vista in the
> distance, an entrancing sunset – words cannot describe it.
> European man was returning to mythology, his sylvan
> paradise.... Wonderful people once lived here. They lived
> their days from morn to night in happiness and innocence.
> The groves rang with their gay singing; the great
> abundance of unspent vigour was poured into love and
> simple joy. The sun bathed these islands and the sea in
> beams, and rejoiced in its lovely children. What a
> marvellous dream, such a sublime illusion ! This is the
> most improbable of all dreams, yet it is on this dream

that mankind has always lavished its powers; it is for this dream that they have made every kind of sacrifice, died on the cross or as prophets; without it nations cannot live, but neither are they able to die.

Nothing could be more startling than the contrast between this and the ugliness of what Stavrogin has just revealed, or the horror of the retributive vision that follows. On the surface it might seem like a crudely ironic device, to throw the evil possibilities of human nature into perspective. However, the myth of 'the Golden Age, has its place among Dostoevsky's Messianic fantasies; he returned to the identical tale in *A Raw Youth*; and its hold on his imagination seems more important than that of a 'sublime illusion'. Or is it merely that the recurrence of the myth records one of the perennial fantasies that return to mock mankind with the promise of an earthly happiness eternally unfulfilled – a use of myth in its most literal and dismissive sense?

Any attempt to account for the ultimate meaning, or the hold of the myth of the Golden Age on Dostoevsky's imagination would perhaps gain very little from any further knowledge of the author's specific views or intentions. It is to the central rôle of the visual image, to the use of imagining itself that attention is directed. Certainly the importance of visual imagery to Dostoevsky is well known from his response to the 'Corpse of Christ' by Holbein the Younger which he had seen in the Kunstmuseum in Basle, and which produced a 'shattering impression, and he stood before it awe-stricken. . . .' The experience is possibly transcribed in *The Idiot* in a conversation between Myshkin and Rogozhin. Yet in neither case is there anything that we would want to call an aesthetic response. He is wholly involved with the subject matter – in the case of Acis and Galatea with an invented subject matter for which the painting has merely suggested the ground. The myth of the

Golden Age is powerfully present: the 'beginnings of mythology, the sylvan paradise . . .' the mixture of the improbable and necessary, 'without [which] nations cannot live' – all make a claim for the overwhelming importance of the dream in the psychic life of mankind.

In one aspect the message is clear enough: myth is the embodiment of human aspiration and its appropriate imaginative form. Yet its status is clouded by ambiguity. What is the relation of the dream to the world of ugliness in Stavrogin's heart? What to the presumed holiness of Tikhon? Where in the conflicting pattern of political doctrine, religious intensities and human monstrosities can such a dream be imagined to fit? In a sense it is not followed up but merely presented – as in the somewhat analogous dream in *The Brothers Karamazov* where the joy of the marriage feast in Cana of Galilee confronts and supplants the horror of the corruption of Zossima's body. Nothing is said about it; it speaks for itself. Yet what does it 'say' beyond the simple fact that it is there, that it is simply a dream of which mankind is capable? The difficulties in any attempt to make it 'say' something, to work it into an appropriate context, appear in 'The Dream of a Ridiculous Man' where the corruption of the Golden Age dream is both assimilated to a conventional notion of 'the Ages of Man', yet ingeniously turned into a form of personal guilt.

Even if Dostoevsky's treatment of those moments of vision which objects of art had suggested to him is based on substance rather than visual form, it still matters that it is a question of images drawn from such a source. The images have a power; the image-making capacity takes its place among the forms of significant discourse – makes a comment on the human situation that is in some way *sui generis*, yet which parallels and is equal to the other languages through which speculation and experience are conveyed. What measures are there to such an equivalence? In what sort of equilibrium do these multiple languages exist? No rationale is given. We are simply confronted with the fact of such a coexistence, from which we must draw the implications, if any, for ourselves. To what extent is a story an answer to an argument, a tale the appropriate completion of a broken-off questioning? There is a considered, if still ambiguous, model in Plato's dialogues where the argument may break off abruptly in favour of a 'myth'. Stewart believed that in studying Plato's myths he was pursuing Plato the mystic rather than Plato the logician. But this now looks like a naïve distinction. The obvious complementarity seems less to imply a total opposition of two modes of discourse than a reciprocity of function in the intention to persuade, an acceptance that two types of explanation cooperate in the same intellectual undertaking.

This is not, of course, to imply that Stavrogin's dream is in any sense an explanation of anything – I shall come later to the problems of any explanatory uses of myth. Rather it is an indication of an imaginative possibility, a claim for the rôle of imagination in the totality of human affairs: partial, fragmentary, uncertain in its implications, but a claim. As such it is one paradigm for the modern literary consciousness in its effort to find an appropriate relation of imagining to whatever beliefs such imaginings may require. It will have some quite precise equivalents in modern literature, with perhaps the closest resemblances in two dream sequences in Thomas Mann: the classical Golden Age which turns to a world of the violent and monstrous, for Aschenbach in *Death in Venice* and, in *The Magic Mountain*, when Hans Castorp falls asleep in the snow.

It is of course important that all of these are dreams, and through the dream the presence of myth in the human consciousness receives its due form of inverted commas. Yet while limitations may be so implied the very unpredictable and arbitrary quality of the dream frees the author from the sense of context which normally controls his intentions. It has the look of something simply and gratuitously given. Nevertheless, the case suggests much of the extended use which the following century has given to an awareness of myth. Stavrogin's dream represents one, perhaps the simplest or most direct, of those formulations by means of image and narration that approach the human situation through a 'poetic logic', for which Plato perhaps once, and later Vico, understood that the essential form of expression was in myth.

2 Meanings and expectations

But what then is myth? Most definitions exist at a very high level of generality, and an admission of the multiple nature of the subject is built into them. There is usually agreement on the factor of narrative. 'Myth is narrative, irrational . . . and comes to mean any anonymously composed story telling of origins and destinies, the explanation a society offers its young of why the world is and why we do as we do, its pedagogic images of the nature and destiny of man' (Warren and Wellek). Or, 'Myth is to be defined as a complex of stories – some no doubt fact, and some fantasy – which, for various reasons, human beings regard as demonstrations of the inner meaning of the universe of human life' (Alan Watts). Others assign such a multiplicity of causes as to be almost completely meaningless: 'Myth is a universal cultural phenomenon originating in a plurality of motives and involving all mental faculties' (David Bidney). Still others wish to establish the character of myth as an imaginative language in its own right: 'An autonomous form of the human spirit, with its own structure, function, expression . . . with unity of feeling' (Cassirer). Or, 'A myth . . . is a schema of the imagination which, independently of the scientific status of the proposition it may subtend, is capable of effectively organizing our way of viewing portions of the external world in accord with its distinctions' (Joseph Margolis).

These are ponderous specimens, and raise difficulties of differing kinds, some of which will return to us rather more grounded in context. But their range, variety and differing levels of generality suggest the scope of the problems that exist in what is still a more traditional and restricted aspect of the concept. Even within those terms of analysing this traditional sense we can feel the overlapping uses of the words 'myth', 'mythology', 'legend', 'folklore', 'tale', even 'story' – and it has often been thought that they should be carefully distinguished from each other. The difficulties of this appear in Professor Kirk's book on myth when he sets out to distinguish between myth and folktale, or as he some-times puts it, between myth and legend, largely on the basis of the roots that 'legend or saga' may have had in actuality. But this is difficult to sustain. The gods of Homer may belong to myth, and may represent in the *Iliad* 'the metaphysical aspect of a primarily legendary narrative', but it is hard to deny that the heroes belong to the world of myth as well. The 'trickster' figure may be described as a standard folklore motif, and yet Kirk's own catalogue of 'commonest themes in Greek [mainly heroic] myths' is led by the entry 'Tricks, riddles, ingenious solutions to dilemmas'. Kirk sees the complexity of the material, the contradictory nature of many particular cases, and realizes that there is no clear dividing line. Yet some distinction needs to be made, and in the end the distinguishing feature of 'myth' seems to be its serious-ness. The term 'myth' is honorific; the 'folktale' is a slighter thing. Of course no fixed criteria for such a classification could be given, and with a change of context or artistic treatment a particular theme could change category.

What is more important, however, is that the grounds for this have nothing to do with the ethnographic or literary material, or with any natural divisions seen in it. The attempt to suggest that there is a basis in the way such people as the Hausa 'distinguish saga-type tales from imaginative myths' is impossible to follow up as this distinction is so easily conflatable with others, and is quite as confusing as anything that tries to discriminate between sacred and non-sacred. And anyway, 'imaginative' loads the dice. It is the very recognition of the rôle of imagination that suggests how the concept 'myth' has been transformed, and in accounting for the transformation in what follows I shall abandon the futile effort to capture the elusive essence of the concept. It is more interesting to examine the variety of uses to which modern writers, not only anthropologists, but philosophers and critics, novelists and poets, have put it.

Myth is one of the oldest elements of the human heritage, but the subject of my study is essentially modern. The ancient world and the Renaissance were concerned with myth, but the nature of their concern was different. Although Plato may have understood some of the ways in which a story could be related to argument and employed myth in a strangely modern sense, he also attacked the stories of the gods as untrue and unworthy of gods. The myths of the cave, of Atlantis, or of Er may involve features of traditional folklore and of free invention, but they are ultimately used as a kind of extended and metaphorical explanation which is an integral part of the overall argument. This sense of the possibilities of myth is probably unique in the ancient world. When Aelius Theon derides the Medea legend it is on the ground of its psychological improbability. Theon seems largely concerned with literal truth and falsehood, with a common-sense criterion of what will and what will not work, and Eliade remarks of his analysis that 'this is more than a devastating critique of the myth; it is a critique of any imaginary world, levelled in the name of simplistic psychology and an elementary rationalism'. Pindar and Virgil and the tragic poets might find profound poetic uses for the relics of the past, but most ancient consideration of myth is strangely literal, as in Euhemerus' account of myth as muddled history.

If ancient commentators were concerned with whether or not the stories of the gods were really so, those of the Renaissance, working within a Christian frame of reference, knew that they could not be literally true. The question for them became: 'What do the tales of the ancient gods represent? What kind of truth lies hidden in stories which cannot be true in the terms that they themselves put?' To represent something was to become the mask for a truth, either occult or abstract. So myth became the subject of allegorical interpretation, which in turn was rationalized with more and more complexity. Seznec describes the academic development of myth studies in the sixteenth century: 'Increasingly erudite and diminishingly alive, less and less felt but more and more intellectualized – such, from now on it seems, is to be the inescapable evolution of mythology.'

A further degree of distance separates the modern curiosity. Rather than 'is it literally true?', or 'what kind of hidden truth might it contain?', the characteristically modern question is one of what meaning the very existence of myth postulates, and might be put for many writers as 'what place does the phenomenon of myth occupy among the languages of mankind?' There are difficulties in such a formulation: certainly the word 'language' is used in a loose and itself characteristically modern way and I shall later return to the problem of the status of such a language. And the word 'myth' as a substantive is itself of comparatively recent origin, appearing in French in 1811 (Robert), in German in 1815 (Grimm), in English in 1830 (*OED*), while in Italian the word 'favola' is still in use from Vico to Leopardi. The modernity of the word may tell us something about the consciousness of myth in its historical context, while merely concealing the complexity of both expectation and usage. It is of some importance that it appears at just the moment when Romantic and nationalist sensibility is joined to a new awareness of the past, and 'myth' has certain affinities with the 'spirit of the age', of nation and tribe, as well as with forms of belief more poetic than literal. But the word 'myth' itself has become a palimpsest. At least in terms of its accumulated associations if not through the continuity of its history, and we have in it now the newest surface on a palimpsestic ground – probably the most plastic and adaptable form of an ancient concept reworked to modern ends.

An important example of the power that the concept of myth has gained through this curious adaptability may be seen in the way it has come to be used in the analysis of social and political change. Consider three cases:

> All societies rest on myths. To justify a particular view of a particular society one needs to identify its basic myths and to reflect upon their impact on the current generations. (Peter Calvocoressi)

> [For Durkheim] . . . the function of myths is to bind a society, create a structure governed by rules and habits. . . . For Sorel, myths are something very different. Their function is not to stabilize, but to direct energies and inspire action. They do this by embodying a dynamic vision of the movement of life, the more potent because not rational, and therefore not subject to criticism and refutation by university wiseacres. A myth is compounded of images that are 'warmly coloured', and affect men not as reason does, nor as education of the will, nor the command of a superior, but as ferment of the soul which creates enthusiasm and incites to action, and, if need be, turbulence. Myths need have no historical reality; they

direct our emotions, mobilize our will, give purpose to all
that we are and do and make.   (Isaiah Berlin)

Myth does not deny things, its function on the contrary
is to speak of them; quite simply it purifies them and
makes them innocent, fixes them in nature and eternity,
gives them a clarity which is not that of explanation but
of statement: if I consider French imperialism as a fact
requiring no explanation, I am very close to finding it
natural, proceeding from itself. So reassuring. In passing
from history to nature myth makes a saving: it abolishes
the complexity of human action, gives it an elemental
simplicity; it suppresses all dialectic or anything which
takes us beyond the immediately visible; it organizes a
world without contradictions because without depth, a
world displayed in the obvious. Myth creates a happy
clarity: things give the appearance of meaning something
in their own right.   (Roland Barthes)

Some presuppositions seem the same. 'Myth' is, at varying
levels of consciousness and degrees of articulateness, a way
of describing the foundations of social behaviour. But the
connotations and claims differ, and the term is used at
different levels of abstraction. The first is the most general.
Societies depend in some fundamental way upon an elusive
and indefinite body of beliefs, many of them not wholly
conscious or susceptible of precise formulation, but which
are crucial to any sense a society may have about itself.
There is an obvious corollary: the identification of the myth
is the art of catching the essence of a situation, of putting
one's finger on the heart of the matter. This may seem to beg
some questions such as the means or criteria of identification. And stated with this simplicity it may seem so vaguely
put as to have a doubtful meaning. But this is because 'myth'
has become a kind of intellectual shorthand which has
gained acceptance as standing for an elusive, almost

unanalysable amalgam of beliefs, attitudes and feelings. The very unapproachability of the content of myth has created the utility of the term and guaranteed its widespread usefulness. With no theoretical implications the term is taken as given.

The commentary on Sorel argues for something narrower. The implied contrast is with Durkheim's view of the social utility of myth which would have closer affinities with the first example (if also a more developed explanation). For Sorel myth is the incarnation of those marvellous and special forces that move men to the most extraordinary accomplishments – a mysterious spring of creativity like the Bergsonian *élan vital*. Some such myth underlies the great movements of history, the Reformation or the French Revolution, and is felt in any great social upheaval or transformation. The great interest in this use lies in the emphasis on the irrational or even sub-rational character of myth, as the form through which energies of an almost biological kind find social effectiveness.

For Roland Barthes it is the exact opposite. Myth in our own society is the a-political language through which the enemy class, the bourgeoisie, beguiles itself and its victims. It freezes the possibility of analysis, reflection and change into the images that deny them. To Barthes 'myth is not defined by the object of its message but by the fashion in which it presents it. There may be formal limits to myth but not ones of substance. So anything may be a myth? Yes, I think so.' Then any aspect of human life can be given the sterilizing form of myth, that specialization which turns expressive speech into bemusing fixation. A phrase, a processed foodstuff, an image in *Paris Match*, a song, the smile on Garbo's face – all may take their place among our myths. But the very universality with which such a fashion of presentation may be applied opens the way to satirical treatment, and a writer in *Le Figaro* finds pleasure in deriding the solemn analysis in a paper set by a provincial professor on the myth of *pommes frites* among the French. And in doing so it is exactly the elasticity of the term which is in question.

Yet Barthes has cast this form of image making in a clearly describable, if dangerously extended, social rôle. And his implicit aim of liberating the mind from seduction by bourgeois devices has some affinity with the Popperite contempt for those irrational notions that have led mankind into the ugliness of political extremism, or the folly of believing that persuasive ideologies are the solution for anything. Here the conventional sense of 'it's a myth', that is a falsehood, retains a degree of vitality. However it seems more a moral sensibility than a category of language that provides the defining element, and the semiotic system converts such sensibilities into the fatality of linguistic forms.

This discussion may seem to move away from the literary uses of myth but it is important in two ways. The first is that in many literary contexts the force of the term comes from the very existence of these cognate uses. It is exactly the extra-literary kind of claim upon which so much literary use depends. And in a fashion quite other than that defined by Barthes these claims are largely ones of substance, however elusive the content may seem. Social beliefs, of course, may parallel, complement or conflict with beliefs of other kinds, with none of them held in an exclusive or formal tidiness. It is perhaps for this reason that some of the most traditional sense in which a society may try to capture its own identity is through its great writers. Homer was 'the education of Hellas', and one may think of the rôle of Goethe in shaping the self-awareness of the German nation. In what is perhaps even a more self-conscious age, when the search for identity has taken more diffuse and tortuous forms, what literature does is even more entangled with those psychological, social or political considerations on which a sense of self or social order may be based. 'Myth' serves a multiple cause. And in the final chapter I shall look further at these forms of service.

The second is connected with the very difficulty of writing about the subject. The degree of overlap in usages, the way in which contexts are subtly altered, or even the relative appropriateness of several meanings to the same context, show the difficulty of controlling the connotations of the word 'myth', not only from one occasion to another but on any one occasion where complex or many-sided demands are made. As the argument advances, its grounds are altered. Sense of context may be the best control we have, but it is seldom a precise one. It is easy to doubt that the working boundaries of such a concept may ever be drawn; our best resource is a cultivated vigilance as to the shifting of the sands. Take that most elastic 'myth of' locution which lends itself to such various degrees of particularity and weight. We move easily from 'the myth of the Eternal Return' to 'the myth of the Long March' to 'the myth of Marilyn Monroe'. Multiplication of differences both in type and degree could easily be shown.

This sense of variable weightings, from profound to quite frivolous, from the Golden Age to B.B. or James Dean, complicates the earlier suggestion about distinguishing between myth and folktale on the grounds of seriousness. The particular ambiguity arises from confronting the more traditional anthropological study of myth with its modern metaphorical extension. Others abound. The distinction between myth and other forms of symbolism is one of them, as both words elude precise definition and overlap in terms of function. The critics who have employed such notions have often been appropriately careless of such considerations in their pursuit of the sense of some work of literature and their effort to convey its wider meaning. Just as they are equally vague about the distinction between the conscious use of myth, and the 'discovery' of it in some underlying pattern which the author could not possibly have intended. And indeed the failure to distinguish in the case of narrative itself between the more traditional sense of the sacred (whatever that may mean) tale, linked in whatever fashion to ritual practices and the prehistory of a society, and the utterly modern sense of simply a significant story or expressive form, will recur in many guises. I shall not only be compelled to accept the full consequences of the ambiguities involved, but to find in them a large measure of the very *raison d'être* of the concept. And I hope that 'significant story' is not merely a begging of questions, but that it is an accurate transcribing of that mixture of vague and urgent intent which has made certain forms of imagining into metaphorical substitutes for other forms of explanation. Above all I am dealing with a modern situation and a modern word, representing a multiplicity of pressures and demands, themselves the keys to the senses of myth they have called into being.

3 *Some theoretical accounts*

Several aspects of the theory of myth are important for the relation of myth to literature, for some of the accounts of what myth *is* have conditioned the uses to which it has been put by writers and critics, and the rôle it has come to occupy in imaginative life. Two things seem important in accounting for particular myths or bodies of myth. One lies in exploring 'what the myth says' and the other in relating 'what the myth says' to how it is seen to function in terms of the particular human society from which it comes. Of course these are not strictly separable, although there may be a difference between concentration on literary or on ethnographic materials. A more general query lies beyond these: having regard for what a thing has meant in a particular place and time, we must go on to ask what is implied by the function, structure or underlying cause. Much of the consideration of these issues sticks more closely than not to the more traditional sense of the term. The theories of myth are of many kinds, and I shall simply sketch four of them in the most brutally simplified way, selected as different (but not exclusive) types of explanation: 1 functionalist, 2 psychological, often psychoanalytic, 3 religious, and 4 theories of symbolic form. These are not all theories in precisely equivalent senses, but I hope to approach through them those differing aspects of myth theory that are relevant to literary study. And I shall later have some comment on the utility of any form of unitary explanation. Part of the point here is to examine the different rôles that have been attributed to myth. To what extent is in explanatory? How much is it primitive philosophizing? How much is it an all-important if hardly definable expressive device for the human psyche?

Functionalism describes myth in terms of its operation within a social structure, often in connection with a ritual which marks a stage in the development or progress of the individual through his life-cycle : birth, initiation, marriage, death – or whatever stages a society may choose to mark. In a sense myth, in this account of it, is not so much a form of saying as of doing; it is less explanatory in a conceptual sense than the verbal accompaniment which gives a vague frame of reference to an activity. The problem that arises from this view is the nature of the verbal accompaniment, and how explanatory it really is. Writers such as Malinowski deny that myths provide overall explanations analogous to those of a scientific or philosophical kind. But they also claim that myths 'come into play when rite, ceremony, or a social or moral rule demands justification'. And justification might easily reach to quite abstract forms of explanation. Even the use of myth as a social device requires full explanation. According to Radcliffe-Brown 'A society depends for its existence on the presence in the minds of its members of a certain system of sentiments by which the conduct of the individual is regulated in conformity with the needs of society.' The use of myth to mould such sentiments would be inconceivable if it did not involve some measure of 'justification'.

An important feature of the functionalist approach is the limitation of myth to its context. The function proceeds from the particular occasion, hence the 'meaning' of the myth is controlled by that occasion or others like it. This limitation to the particular circumstance means that both generalization and comparative study are extremely suspect. Such an attitude is at least in part an empiricist reaction against the excessive generality and the hypothetical character of nineteenth-century theorizing which saw in myth a single underlying pattern – say, of solar origin. It can be seen that a rigorous functionalism would not lend itself easily to the literary imagination, and perhaps its most important influence in that respect has been the close connection of myth with ritual. For ritual has hardly been distinguished from myth by many literary critics. The identification of ritual patterns in fiction – say initiation rituals in Hemingway or Faulkner, or the sacrifice of the scapegoat in *Tender is the Night* – is treated in exactly the same way as the discovery of some underlying 'myth'. The connection between the two terms is left happily obscure, and Wheelwright offers material drawn largely from ritual (especially from Van Gennep's *Les Rites de passage*) to show the character of the 'mythopoeic outlook'.

Psychological theories are based on the supposition of some universal characteristics of the human psyche which may be revealed through myth, such as Freud's postulation of the incest taboo and the primary rôle of the Oedipal conflict. The source of this in Freud is almost biological: one starts with the hypothesis of an instinct, and the repression of that instinct becomes the basis of a theory of culture. This has been extended to many considerations involving cultural and social behaviour, with the unconscious impulses and repression speaking through the symbolic language of dreams, a language which throughout its history mankind has sought to capture in myth, ritual and art. It is impossible to do justice to Freud's rich, complex and highly inventive response to myth. Some of it borders on a fictional anthropology, such as the rôle of the father in primitive societies, or notions of the 'primal horde'. Otherwise it is concerned with the exploration of particular symbols drawn from the mythical and presumably unconscious past. The importance of all this for thinking about literature may be enormous, but the attempt to use those basic Freudian notions that hypothetically should underlie both myth and art in criticism is almost universally disappointing, producing critical observations that are mechanical, Procrustean and dull. In *Concepts of Criticism* Wellek speaks wryly of the psychoanalytic school, particularly of one Arthur Wormhoudt, who sees breasts in hills and for whom the act of writing is the spilling of mother's milk. It is one of the paradoxes of literary history that a concept containing such a profound insight, appealing so powerfully to the imagination, should have led to critical work which is largely of very poor quality.

The Jungian theory of archetypes, however dubious its ground, has perhaps fared better as a device for literary analysis. For Jung the archetypes are transcendental symbolic forms found universally in the psychic life of man, embodied in a collective unconscious in which the individual psyche unknowingly participates. In dreams, myths, magic, ritual and art these forms reveal themselves, and their repetition lends itself to comparative study, so that the fundamental features of our accumulated experience and feeling may be seen in terms of the total human inheritance, the formal outlines, continuity and coherence of which can, thanks to such symbolism, be effectively traced. There is an anti-rationalism implicit in all this, and 'the fund of uncommon images which fatally confuse the mental patient' is also 'the matrix of a mythopoeic imagination which has vanished in our rational age'. And 'Myth is the actual and indispensable stage between conscious and unconscious cognition.' So myth has a vital rôle in Jung's picture of the mind, and as such has lent itself easily to the students of the unconscious levels that may be found in literature – the 'underthought'. Yet the 'collective unconscious' is pure hypothesis of the sort which is inaccessible to empirical investigation. Furthermore, in the interpretation of myths, as of dreams, there is a startling freedom for 'seeing-as'. A symbol may fit the requirements of a wide variety of hypothetical explanations, and if there is no empirical form of test the criteria for deciding on the best account will be impossible to give. Unless we simply judge in terms of the overall coherence of the account, and the criteria for 'coherence' may be subjective – even 'literary'.

Jung's theories might be considered in either of two ways: either as a commentary on the forms man has devised in the course of his cultural history, or as a key to an occult or supernaturally derived spiritual life. In the latter sense they become versions of the religious views of myth. But shorn of the problem of what their origin may be, or what ultimate meaning may be implicit in them, the Jungian archetypes have proved adaptable to some critical purposes, especially in suggesting the relation of literary symbols in particular works to larger categories, and so have helped define multiple types of affinity or difference in literary genres.

Another study of myth which might be accounted a

psychological study is that found in the works of Lévi Strauss. I shall have reason to return to them in another context, but if I understand his claims correctly, they too are based upon the use of myth to reveal certain characteristics of the functioning of the human mind. However these are not to be found as they are for Freud in the symbolic representation of conflict but at a further degree of abstraction. The comparative study of large numbers of myths show similarities of structure, which through diagrammatic and algebraic analysis of the structure of structures, may be shown to relate in some as yet unspecified way to organic features of the brain itself. The principle of opposition sets up a binary system which proposes a model for the resolution of conflict, and is seen both in the products of the mind working towards that resolution and in its very structure.

This has been one of the most severely criticized features of his extensive study of myth, partly because the relation of verbal evidence to organic conclusion rests on hypotheses which are as yet impossible to conceive, partly because on many occasions when he should by his own reckoning be talking about structure he is actually talking about content. And in practice the 'algebra of relations' seems a distant fantasy, the dream of a structural key to the mind itself taking second place to the detailed description of the place of myth among the multiple expressive languages of mankind.

It is in fact not the theoretical conclusion, attainable or not, that has given Lévi-Strauss his extraordinary importance as a student of myth, but the enormous range of comparisons, the suggestion of the persistence of certain model relationships, and the notion of the myth as mediator between man and the inhuman facts of existence. It is the notion of the universality of myth and the distinctiveness of its function in societies that seem utterly remote from one another, that is more impressive than the abstract formulae.

And behind this lies the notion that myth conceals a message, is a code to be broken in order to unfold the inner meaning. The appeal of Lévi-Strauss to students of literature may lie less in the value of the structural models of the relations between the elements of various myths than in the analogies between the decoding of the myth and methods of critical interpretation. However, the current literary uses of structuralism depend more directly on structural linguistics, from which Lévi-Strauss himself derives so much.

By *religious* theories I shall indicate, perhaps somewhat too vaguely, the view of those writers who claim that the 'language' of myth has some reference beyond its more obvious source in human affairs, that one must identify as some kind of metaphysical or religious foundation. This is a class of explanation to which it is very hard to give any clear form, but which takes in a variety of views from the wholly occult to the vaguest possible sense of the further implications of myth. When a writer like Joseph Campbell claims 'Myth is the picture language of metaphysics', or Mircea Eliade that 'the foremost function of myth is to *reveal* [my italics] the exemplary for all human rites and all human activities', one feels the pull of a commitment which is powerful but not explicit. 'Reveals' suggests an authority, 'metaphysics' some replies to ultimate questions. The status of this commitment is ambiguous, and such writers are often elusive, their religious implications syncretic, creating an image of a world religion which lies behind the particular instances of known religions, a world religion which speaks through the symbolic language of myth, hinting at the universal truth through each of its forms. ('The fundamental form and the playful manifestation' – Heinrich Zimmer.) Yet this ambiguity seems part of the very mentality that these mythographers exemplify; a literal sense of the religious dimension of life is simply not the way in which the dimension works: '. . . it must be conceded, as a basic principle of our natural history of gods and heroes, that whenever a myth has been taken literally its sense has been perverted' (Joseph Campbell). So the hidden god remains hidden, and the symbolic language of myth remains untranslatable into other languages.

At least largely so. For to insist on the total untranslatability of the symbolic language is to make it accessible only to the mystic or the initiate – as much of the occult tradition has always insisted. Of course, this hardly answers the case, for the full implication would be to make comparative study impossible. An uncrossable line would be drawn between the total mystery and the place of myth in those forms of art and literature that must claim to some form of participation in an intelligible world. What I have called 'religious' may not be religious in the strict sense but, in concerning themselves with the claims which the content of myth may have, such theories point to fundamental problems concerning the nature of belief, and put in question the indeterminate rôle which myth has come to play for the modern imagination.

Throughout this discussion I have made a number of references to myth as symbolic language, or as a kind of *symbolic form*, which has seemed to be implicit in theories that I have mentioned. And I should say something of those theories that speak of myth as a self-contained symbolic language. (How are we to decipher the content of that language, and to discover what the existence of such a language may imply for our other modes of thought?) In these cases, partly to reach a further level of generality, the word 'myth' is used in a wider sense than in the immediately preceding theories. And this is exactly because they are concerned with more abstract conceptions than other theories may employ, even if not in any very fully articulated form.

One possible manner of approach is to work towards the

essential character of myth by isolating it from other forms of language. There is a variety of 'symbolic forms', to use a term that has its principal authority in Cassirer, of which myth is a large, self-contained, autonomous body, with no explanatory value outside itself, yet which has a truth intelligible in its own mode contained within it. In Cassirer the theory is worked out in immense detail, yet it is faced by serious difficulties. One is analogous to that of the religious theory. If myth is a self-contained and non-referential symbolic structure, how then do we describe what it is about? It is said to be an embodiment of expression of human feeling, and thus a symbolic language of feeling, expressing the unity and continuity of experience. Yet the truth to be found in such a symbolic language is subjective and psychological, a pattern of belief which may have the socially and humanly valuable function of creating an inner equilibrium, and in creating through the myth (as in the functionalist view) a relation between the self and the social order. But here again, the status of such a belief creates unresolved ambiguities. One may indicate certain things about the forms through which symbolic language works, but what it says or claims has no validity beyond the pure function of dealing with human aspirations, hopes and fears. This comes close to the treatment of myth as a theory of fictions, yet its character might be undermined by the acceptance of its wholly fictional nature. What remains in myth is a series of forms, like the objects in a museum, a testimony to inner needs, a language to whose existence we may point, but which in an ultimate sense we can never read.

There is a mixture in all these theories of a desire to give an adequate explanation of the phenomenon of myth and to evaluate its place in the whole spectrum of human thought. Yet however different the manner of it, for all of them myth fulfils its rôle precisely because it is non-rational, indeterminate, and uncertain in the nature of its ultimate claims. If its precision of function in its original context is dependent on this very lack of rational tidiness, what are the implications for the student of myth? Here the points of view divide, with some writers clearly committed to an occult view of mystery for its own sake, and others to the place of myth as evidence in a rational scientific enterprise. The difference between these approaches and the study of the affinities of myth and literature will emerge in my final chapter.

It is worth asking here what constitutes a 'theory' of myth, as the difficulties in any unitary explanation, either genetic or formal, are enormous. And the definitions we saw in the last section are so elastic as to suggest that a single account would strain the limits of what we think a theory ought to do. In this section the issues have been simplified by the omission of the wider extensions of the term. This difficulty is shown clearly in Kirk's final chapter:

> There is no single type of myth – that has been amply confirmed in earlier chapters – and unitary theories of mythical function are largely a waste of time; but that does not mean that there may not be a primary mode of mythical imagination or expression which is then applied in different ways and to different ends.

Here the very phrases 'type of myth', unity of function, 'primary mode of mythical imagination' seem to speak to frames of reference of quite different kinds. And the typology he then suggests, which separates the narrative, operative and explanatory functions, is akin to saying that any myth can be seen in a variety of non-exclusive aspects. This seems perfectly all right so long as the movement from 'type of myth' to 'mythical imagination' is not just a dismissing of the problem. In fact a 'theory' of the 'mythical imagination' would be a very different sort of thing from the theories of function that he has been discussing. And while it might be agreed that this problem is more fundamental, Kirk has no real contribution to make to it.

It is certainly to this sense of 'mythical imagination' that literary study must turn, but hardly in the Cassirer sense of isolating the mythical as a separate and self-contained category of the imagination. Rather I shall try to describe the interplay of myth with other forms of imagining, to examine its rôle in modern sensibility and literary thought, both in creative work and in critical interpretation.

4 The uses of myth

A general claim about the place of myth in literature makes all of the ambiguities of the matter apparent: 'A study of the great literary classics shows that their themes are organically interwoven with mythic and religious belief' (Harry Slochower). It is perhaps most useful to begin simply by examining the senses in which the terms here might be employed; certainly it is the sort of remark which cries out for some context which will make its terms intelligible. Are 'mythic' and 'religious' carefully discriminated and complementary terms, or are they a mere lumping together of matters thought to have fundamental affinities? In an essay principally concerned with Kafka and Mann the 'classics' are principally represented by Dante, Racine's *Phèdre*, Wagner's *Ring*, Blake, and Melville's *Moby-Dick*. Aside from the obvious slant to a picture of the classics that such a list implies, even in these cases 'myth' and 'religious belief' would be different things, and 'organically interwoven' would have totally different implications. Take the case of Dante, where myth and belief would have to be distinguished if the terms are to be intelligible. For Dante's rich and complex use of what is undoubtedly myth, even to the extent of being borrowed from the ancient world, stands in an illustrative relationship to what we normally call his beliefs. Would we therefore wish to say that the Christian allegory was part of the organic whole conveying the whole design of Christian belief, while the 'myth' is a super-added embellishment? But if one speaks of the 'Catholic myth' of Dante the modern sense of the word embraces, loosely, both of these aspects. In the particular case it is hard to know whether there is a calculated looseness of this kind, or simply the habitual haphazardness that modern ambiguities seem to allow.

Here, as in any other case where we may distinguish myth and belief it would be easy to see, as far as the Christian faith is concerned, what 'organically interwoven' might mean – mixed metaphor though it may be – since all forms of Western literature exist in the shadow of the Christian faith and could hardly escape from a use of its language. Hence it is easy to show that Shakespeare is in some sense a Christian; whatever his religious views might have been he could hardly have avoided using a vocabulary and some elements of a conceptual scheme that have a Christian source. The 'degree' speech in *Troilus* has a theological basis, however it may relate to the meaning of that work. Yet to show that *Troilus* or *Lear* or *Measure for Measure* have some specific and intelligible form of Christian message is quite another matter. Many points of reference reflect a complex and sometimes conflicting background of 'belief' without containing the play. And 'organically interwoven' has very limited implications for whatever it is the work in question might really be about.

With 'myth' the case is quite different. We may feel that *The Tempest* lends itself to mythical interpretation, although it is informed by no particular myth. We may argue for fertility cults, death by water, ritual reconciliation, but whatever validity these may have they are extrapolations at one or two degrees' remove from the play. Such mythical interpretations of course do not mean that Shakespeare had any such things in mind for they are historicized notions which he could not possibly have conceived. But supposing some degree of corresponding intention were involved, did he use the 'myth' of Troilus for the play of that name? Or merely the 'story'? And what would the difference be between the two? An analogous problem exists for *Phèdre*. If the myth has been borrowed from Euripides, is it the *same* myth? And what would we mean by 'same'? Do we feel the same forces working through both plays? And what place would that sense in the *Hippolytus* of terrible and malign deities have in the Christian world of Racine? Valéry has said that 'fille de Minos et de Pasiphaë' is not a genealogical statement, and we can feel the curious energy of evocation that the old legend creates in the line, although its very distance is part of what it evokes. And the almost self-contradictory nature of 'organically interwoven' might begin to express the difficulties of Racine's task, of the multiplicity of elements his intensely formal theatre must resolve.

In the case of Wagner's *Ring*, where no element of belief complicates the issue, where the 'myth' is the eclectic and self-conscious product of the Romantic search for identity, we may feel that the words on the page are turgid and pretentious, while the stories stripped of the language have the same interest as any traditional tale. But the musical version is marvellous and wholly transformed. Does the myth really enter when we switch the music on? The music of a Sophocles tragedy is missing, but we do not doubt the presence of whatever power the 'myth' was meant to convey.

I should like to make a broad contrast between the case of the modern author and those authors of the past, Christian and ancient, whose myths were perhaps a more natural inheritance, but for whom the relationship to the material was defined by other factors. With Racine or Milton the mythological frame is an accepted convention, and in *Paradise Lost* the rich deployment of classical mythology comes dangerously close to the sort of embellishment where the familiar references require the stock response, although that response implies a highly civilized pleasure in the reference for its own sake, a form of connoisseurship. And of course, as with Dante, the terms of accommodation with the Christian scheme of things have been meticulously worked out, and it is clear that seventeenth-century syncretism responded to conditions that were exigent in a way unthinkable to our own.

The question arises as to what the Renaissance or Baroque writer expected the most intense evocations of the pagan gods to indicate. The high point of Racine's *Phèdre* might show some relief in an 'otherness', the recognition of an elemental, chthonic force breaking through the official accommodation which Racine's world required of him.

C'est Vénus toute entière à sa proie attachée

gives the extreme moment of self-revelation a grandeur, as well as a vision of the emptied self wholly devoured by the single passion. Do we take Racine's denial that this is the personification of a psychological force as simply a manoeuvre to lessen the guilt of Phèdre and make the play more acceptable? And if we take his preface literally, what is implied? We do not have the terror of real possession by the wholly alien that produced the madness of Pentheus. But of course with the *Bacchae* of Euripides a different relationship of the poet to his material may be presupposed, although the ambiguity of Euripides lies, in part, in his refusal to make clear what value to put on the divine personification. When the gods are monsters and bullies the notorious rationalism of the poet and his critique of the inherited tradition becomes most obvious. As it is in his transformation of the myth into a vehicle of psychological analysis. Yet the portrayals always do justice to the life of the personified divinity and the notion of a simple rationalism will hardly help us with the *Bacchae* – or for that matter, with the *Hippolytus*.

The issue is complex, and the attitude of the ancient world to its myths had passed beyond the point of taking the tales as literally true. But they obviously represented some kind of truth that had not yet been swallowed by the allegorical interpreters. The intention of those who set out to rationalize and moralize the tales of the gods – or of those like Theon who wished to deride them – still came nowhere near the medieval intention where one might have wished to convert the Oedipus tale into allegory. The kind of explanation required had not yet found its vocabulary.

These cases may do no more than suggest something of the variety of what is implicit in attributing some mythical element to a literary work. And of course if we wish to use the term as widely as Barthes any work of literature, by its very existence as a form of speech, will have its mythical dimension. But this very width destroys its critical usefulness. Much closer to the study of literature is the more intentional use of myth as a means of deepening and enriching a poem or narrative. The simplest examples may be drawn from modern literature, where the author has imported and consciously used materials of a traditional mythical kind. With Yeats there is certainly a variety of consciously deployed forms of myth, even if their use is not necessary consistent. They may exist on several levels – the personages from Irish folklore, the more picturesque elements of Platonic philosophy such as 'the great year', or borrowings from the occult. 'Yeats' "Sailing to Byzantium", to take a famous example of the comic vision at random, has the city, the tree, the bird, the community of sages, the geometrical gyre and the detachment from the cyclic world.' All of these bits of mythical apparatus have, for Northrop

Frye, reference to 'archetypes' which relate back to the 'comic vision' as an imaginative whole. Here they may stand for the range of mythical devices concentrated in a single – and great – poem.

But of the many kinds of myth that Yeats employs it is the most obvious and simplest that raises some disturbing questions. To what extent does the presence of the Cuchulain tale – a myth derived from the Irish past – give that imaginative enlargement which is one of its obvious aims? The case of Yeats is somewhat complicated by the fact that the poems that are concerned with folkloric narrative or character belong largely to an earlier period of his work. But when the traditional figure does appear in the mature poem he seems wholly assimilated to an imaginative scheme of the poet's own, and the life of the mythic personage has no more evocative identity than those characters drawn from among the poet's friends, or the wholly fictional characters that he employed:

And I myself created Hanrahan. . . .

The necessary emblematic figure is not only created by his own imagination, but recognized as such. Hanrahan, the Countess Cathleen and others are testimony to the power that the self-created image has over the poet himself, in every respect as authentic and powerful as the Oisin or Cuchulain derived from traditional sources.

Among the possibilities that arise here is simply that the creative power of the particular poet as 'mythmaker' is equal to whatever traditional material he may assimilate and use. But in this, of course, we are not only using the term 'myth' in a double sense, but suggesting it as a measure of value, or of the artist's creative powers. And the question of when a myth works or is effective will depend upon literary criteria and the sense of the particular case. If one asks a question about the effectiveness of the myth itself the

Irish tales provide an ambiguous example. They do not have
the weight of evocation that belongs to so much classical
reference in English poetry. If one compares from the point
of view of myth alone the lines of Milton

> Not that faire field
> Of Enna, where Proserpin gathring flours
> Herself a fairer Floure by gloomie Dis
> Was gathered, which cost Ceres all that pain
> To seek her through the world . . .

with those of Yeats

> The host is riding from Knocknarea
> And over the grave of Clooth-na-Bare;
> Caoilte tossing his burning hair . . .

there is a marked difference of expectation. Part of Yeat's
purpose lies in the very unfamiliarity, the desire to create
out of an unknown body of folklore a coherent myth and
indirectly a national continuity of feeling, a sense of
national identity in depth. This is not a poem of particular
distinction and Yeats's more successful uses of myth are
eclectic and highly personal. The specialized historical
intention may fail and the poem succeed. It is *his* Cuchulain
that is alive for us. While the tales themselves may have
charm or the interest that an anthropologist or psychologist
might find in them – as in Heinrich Zimmer's treatment of
the tale of Conn-edda – it is our own concern with what
Yeats was doing that gives the imaginative reciprocity of
poem and legendary matter its force. What is created is not
a national myth, but an episode in the development of a
great poet.

The very unfamiliarity of a body of myth or legend may
of course be exploited precisely because its distance seems
imaginatively useful, when the claim of the exotic may be
part of the shock tactics of a writer who consciously uses

his mythical material for the effect of contrast. This is at least one of the purposes behind the elaboration of the Quetzalcoatl myth in Lawrence's *The Plumed Serpent*, and the solemn purveyor of myth criticism who says 'there can be no doubt of the value of anthropology in helping us understand Lawrence's novel' clearly does not know where to begin. The pulling together of Aztec fragments, the invention to both religious content and ritual form, have lent themselves to some of the finest unintentional comedy in an author whose work is rich enough in it anyway. But the artistic failure of *The Plumed Serpent* makes its use in evidence interesting, if possibly double-edged. Certainly it is a straightforward example of what Richard Chase calls the 'quest' or 'search' for myth. The urgency of the quest proceeds from the conflicts within our own civilization, and in this case, for Lawrence, from the decadence and enfeeblement of Western life, the deliquescence of Christianity into a form of sentimentalism, the need for some rich and imaginative form of life in a world grown pale, mechanical and abstract. The second edge may be found when we ask about the effectiveness of the artist's response, and how we are to explain that sometimes the 'myth' works and other times it does not. Is the fault here in the myth itself? Or in the way that it has been 'realized'? One can see that in Lawrence's case he set himself a problem of the utmost difficulty. The very appropriateness to the spiritual condition Lawrence has diagnosed seems to set for the myth in question a problem of appalling dimensions, and there remains an unbridgeable gap between diagnosis and cure.

The thought that the myth can cure has been widely shared as an aspect of the 'quest' but a tentative one. Chase speaks cautiously of 'the new mythological literature – the work of Eliot, Yeats, Mann, Joyce, Toynbee, Freud and others [which] has been able to make only a few tentative steps.' For one thing Chase's sympathy with the rôle of

myth in creative literature is qualified by his rejection
of the view that 'myth is philosophy – that it is a system of
metaphysical or symbolic thought, that it is a theology, a
body of dogma, a world view, that it is in direct opposition
to science, is indeed the other side of the scientific coin'. The
problem here lies in attempting to separate the imaginative
enterprise from those commitments towards which the
enterprise might be directed. We shall see later some of the
problems in defining a status for the imagination's 'mercies'.
Yet when Chase complains that the modern uses of myth
make of it what it was never meant to be, he presupposes a
view of what it ought to be, and adopts a prescriptive
narrowness of attitude towards modern uses. For it seems
clear enough that many modern writers are using myth in
precisely the way Chase says they should not.

This is so even if an area of calculated vagueness surrounds
the imaginative enterprise. For Yeats and Lawrence are certainly not trying to promote a literal belief in the myths they
have unearthed or created. Nor is Mann seeking to promote a
literal belief in alchemy. To use a myth as an energizing or
ordering principle, and to appeal to the imagination through
it, is to suggest a validity which is in large measure controlled by the context which a work of art provides. At one
level, in the novel at least, the myth is as serious as the
degree to which a character takes it seriously or to which it
has some consequence for that character. But if we ask
about the curative power of the myth, we may feel that in
The Plumed Serpent the demonstration is somewhat forced,
and that the vaguely evocative repetitions, fragments of
song and tag-lines of *Under the Volcano* suggest an artistic
use of the ritualized more effective than that of the 'Mumbo
Jumbo will hoo-doo you' variety. But then, of course the
purpose is not the same. And it is different again with the
other obvious 'Mexican' example, that of Artaud. For his
dissolution of drama into ritual is above all a concern with

dramatic form, and remote from the question of the cure of souls, at least in so far as they can be represented as individual characters. Lawrence in the end seems to be making an indirect claim for the validity of an imaginative and psychological transformation through the powers of myth and ritual which one hopes transcends the particular example.

More indirect, yet in some respects more literal senses of 'cure' are suggested in Mann's *The Magic Mountain*. With the variety of symbolism employed it is hard to say where the 'myth' can be isolated from the whole design, except in Hans Castorp's dream in the snow where a series of literal mythological images represents one of the most intense and concentrated moments in the passage towards self-knowledge. We may be intended to recognize such a passage, marked through the seven years of alembic isolation, yet the conclusion of the process casts some doubt on the efficacy of both myth and magic in the cure of souls. The investigation may be rich in insights which follow upon its tortuous path, but the final transformation, if it can be said to exist at all, is ambiguous in the extreme. The symbolic devices have marked the stages of a spiritual undertaking, enabling Mann to give form to an internal process, yet they seem a fortuitous embellishment and do not indicate the real content or outcome.

This giving of form relates to, if it is not the same as, the structural use of the *Odyssey* story as a framework for Joyce's *Ulysses*, with the mythical tale acting like the mannequin in the shop window upon which all sorts of changing displays may be exhibited, itself suggesting the fundamental human form, and through it the wider uses of the objects displayed. This may imply what some will feel a disparaging critical judgment, yet it is not intended as such. To follow the pattern behind the novel through Stuart Gilbert's useful book, is somewhat – to change the simile – like seeing the mythical skeleton through the living flesh. Yet one must ask to what extent the design once seen gives an associative enrichment to the work as a whole. Do we look back to the Telemacheia and understand Joyce better? In one sense we obviously do in that we see a dimension of Joyce's intention expressed. But the actual light thrown on Joyce's novel by the associative echoes from the Homeric original seems academic and thin, and to think too closely on it is to look away from the richness of what Joyce has created. Yet Eliot saw, in his review of *Ulysses*, that the parallel use of the *Odyssey* has the great importance 'of a scientific discovery' in creating 'a way of controlling, of ordering, of giving a shape and significance to the immense panorama of futility and anarchy which is contemporary history'. He credits Yeats as the first to be conscious of the need for a 'mythical method'. *The Golden Bough* with having concurred to make it possible. And this mythical method is 'a step towards making the modern world possible for art, towards . . . order and form'.

It is worth sorting out what might follow from this. There is of course the primary intention of establishing the effect of myth in the classicizing rôle as the bringer of order and form. But how is it that myth has such an 'order' to which the modern writer can appeal? That there is some order intrinsic to the mythical material itself would seem very unlikely, and Eliot in any case says nothing about it. And even if there were, the choice of the *Odyssey* as an example of such an order would be very odd. Far from being 'myth' in any pure sense it is the conscious artistic reworking of mythical materials by a great artist, and such order as it has is one which that artist has invented. (Even if it is as episodic in much of its structure as a long night out in Dublin.) So rather than a 'mythical method' what is implied is something closer to what Northrop Frye describes as the dependence of literary works on the formal properties of their predecessors. That the further implications of Frye's argument sometimes suggest an infinite regress creates another difficulty but does not affect the particular case. The *Odyssey* provides order just as *Tom Jones* or *The Knight's Tale* or any other carefully designed plot might have done. What the 'mythical' element provides is surely very different. The antiquity, the familiarity, the multiple literary incarnations, of the Odysseus story, the degree to which it has fascinated and involved the European mind, all add something which is not exactly a form of ordering, but which presents openings for the imagination.

It is difficult to tell from rather undeveloped remarks whether Eliot thought of 'making the modern world possible for art' as being identical with, or in some way complementary to, the providing of 'order and form'. The notion that all good literature 'so far as it is good' strives towards classicism becomes confusing, both through the introduction of a value consideration, and through spreading the word 'classical' so thinly that it becomes more or less whatever succeeds. But of course one must accept the argument in its context, recognize the point of Eliot's struggle with an uncomprehending literary public and the importance of claiming that works like *Ulysses* and *The Waste Land* represent an orderly and classical art, not the chaos and confusion of the modern world – that they confront this chaos rather than being part of it.

It is of greater importance to examine the sense of the 'mythical method' through Eliot's own use of it, especially in *The Waste Land*, published in 1922, the year before the essay in question. Two preliminary points should be made. The mythical references in *The Waste Land* may be thematically connected, but they are not parts of a single narrative, myth or group of myths. So they do not provide an ordering set of points of the compass through which to organize one's view of a diverse landscape. In this they differ wholly from the use of the Odysseus tale as Eliot describes it. Second, the particular mythical clue or *point d'appui* seems rich in implications of a kind that the Odysseus frame does not have for *Ulysses*. The Fisher King, the Hanged Man, Death by Water, etc., clearly have a rôle in the poem that the sirens do not have for Joyce. Rather than a parallel narrative indicating a pattern, Eliot's myths – or myth fragments – make spiritual claims, or at least provide the clues to spiritual dimensions. Rather than an ordering frame they define or at least suggest what the poem is about. But they do so with immense ambiguity. If we can assume that the Christian 'mythology' of *Ash Wednesday* or of the *Four Quartets* has some direct (if not literal) claim on our beliefs, what does one make of the note to line 46 of *The Waste Land*?

> I am not familiar with the exact constitution of the Tarot pack of cards from which I have obviously departed to suit my own convenience. The Hanged Man, a member of the traditional pack, fits my purpose in two ways: because he is associated in my mind with the Hanged God of Frazer, and because I associate him with the hooded figure in the passage of the disciples to Emmaus in Part V. The Phoenician Sailor and the Merchant appear later; also the 'crowds of people', and Death by Water is executed in Part IV. The Man with Three Staves (an authentic member of the Tarot pack) I associate, quite arbitrarily, with the Fisher King himself.

This is the most explicit statement that Eliot makes about his use of myth and what stands out is a repeated attitude: 'I have obviously departed', 'to suit my own convenience', 'fits my purpose', 'I associate', 'I associate, quite arbitrarily'. The poet makes clear not only that he will manipulate the elements of myth as he pleases, but will assign to them a meaning of his own choosing. Obviously this choice cannot be wholly the subject of whim or the connotations would become absurdly contradictory, and tearing his materials wholly out of their original sense would make their use pointless. What then of the Fisher King and the Hanged Man? We must of course in the first instance see them as Eliot has situated them, as part of a pattern of allusions playing upon the contrast of fertility and sterility, giving a variety of dimensions to a modern sense of desolation. Does the evocation of the myth take us beyond this into the imaginative country of *The Golden Bough* where the notions of sacrifice, loss and redemption take on a richer meaning through the depths of the human past? The intention may have been realized without doing more than indicating an area of the human spirit, standing in ironic contrast to the modern context which Eliot has created for it. And there may indeed be the further irony that Eliot whose 'search for myth' is presented as a search for order, may in the open-endedness of his use of mythical fragments suggest rather the romantic impulse to explore forever tempting but undefinable depths.

Although Yeats, Joyce and Eliot are the great practitioners, in English at least, of the 'mythical method', they do not in any sense make it 'a' method, or in any identifiable sense 'methodical'. Nor is the 'new mythological literature' limited to them; Chase's own list shows what varied bed-fellowship even a few examples may provide. A catalogue of 'the uses of myth' might, by the multiplication of cases, show no more than the enormous scale on which the modern 'quest for myth' has operated – and would in any case be subject to the vagaries of interpretation. Others, as with these few examples, would show an intentional in-volvement which is very far from having a single model of use. Nor can we step behind the variety of uses to see a single type of motivation. Yet certain common features can be indicated. First, whatever his purpose, point of view or whatever his historical source, for any writer *his* myth is inevitably chosen in response to the spiritual condition of modern man, to the very fact of existence in a post-mythological age. Second, it is a characteristic feature of such an age that no particular body of myth comes to hand naturally. So the modern writer chooses something which is inevitably in some degree alien even if it forms a part of an accepted literary tradition. What is present in Mann's novel of the primitive tale of a man who sold his soul to the devil that is not seen through the rich and marvellous literature of the Faustus legend? Can we separate the 'myth' from its more self-conscious literary versions? In attempting to say how literature *uses* myth one has fallen into the habit of distinguishing between primal stuff and the self-conscious reworkings, as the students of the myths of primitive peoples have felt obliged to do. Although we cannot reasonably say where the notion of 'myth' leaves off and that of 'story' begins, we feel in the most modern, self-conscious usage a groping for something that the 'myth' says and which 'stories' do not.

The kind of confusion to which this may lead is well shown by Ted Hughes's preface to his adaptation of Seneca's *Oedipus*, where he speaks of his wish to create a text

that would release whatever inner power this story, in its plainest, bluntest form, still has, and to unearth, if we could, the ritual possibilities within it. Sophocles' Oedipus would not have been so suitable for this work as Seneca's. The Greek world saturates Sophocles too thoroughly: the evolution of the play seems complete, fully explored and in spite of its blood-roots, fully civilized. The figures in Seneca's *Oedipus* are Greek only by convention: by nature they are more primitive than aboriginals. They are a spider people scuttling among hot stones. The radiant moral world of Sophocles is simply not present here. Seneca hardly notices the intricate moral possibilities of his subject. Nevertheless, while he concentrates on tremendous rhetorical speeches and stoical epigrams, his imagination is quietly producing something else – a series of epic descriptions that echo to the raw dream of Oedipus, the basic, poetic, mythical substance of the fable, and whatever may have happened to the rhetoric, this part has not dated at all.

Here the inner power is contrasted with whatever might be a more 'civilized' rendering, the 'raw dream' with the rhetoric, the culture-bound with 'mythical substance' which never dates. The notion that the 'raw' is alive in a way that the 'civilized' is not would encounter its obvious difficulties if an extended comparison were made of the Sophocles and Seneca plays. It is simply a means for the modern poet of defining his own poetic aims, and capturing for an immediate purpose what he regards as the vitality of his source.

Another casualty here of the search for the mythical is the world of moral discrimination. By implication, of course, it is the other way around: the myth vanishes as the moral world is formed. The modern poet must seek beneath the well-explored and 'radiant' moral world, which may mean in practice the world of complex explanations, reasons and accommodations that man in any civilized context owes to man. In the stuff of the dilemma we find the myth working. A crude contrast and one which would – hardly stand up to the closer inspection of its terms, yet which turns the concept of myth into the suitable short-hand for whatever it is that lies far beneath the surface of our social forms, and which, for better or for worse, only the poet can recover for us. Stavrogin's dream was an escape from inner violence into the natural civility of the Golden Age; the 'raw dream' is a restoration of a primal violence to the slaves of moral and intellectual elaboration.

If by chance one has suggested through the phrase 'the uses of myth' some sense of the derivative, the tradition – and convention – laden notion of a rather comfortable inheritance, Hughes's indication fuses the sense of a remote and terrible past with the notion of a primary creation. This mixture of the fundamental and the creative is part of the currency of the term. 'The poet makes the myth' says Sartre (echoing the terms of the ancient world precisely), and while his intention is to discriminate between certain of the workings of poetry and prose, 'myth' seems to stand for the imaginative dimensions of literature. And this currency is adopted by some writers who are pleading for a more experimental attitude towards the novel. Paul West writes of 'the most alert and attuned and imaginative writers of prose fiction' who 'no longer aim at an informative factuality such as we find in *Père Goriot, Buddenbrooks* etc . . .' but seek to 'create a plasmatic assortment which, at most, initiates myth and, at least, remains with us as a sample of a condition – "reality" – that for the first time we have recognized as *the* condition from which nothing can be excluded'. So much here is uncertain that it is best to avoid comment on the simplistic notion of traditional fiction, on the alternative 'reality', or on the implied doctrine of the imagination. But that the imaginative artist may 'at most, initiate myth' suggests that myth is the supreme vehicle of the creative imagination and stands as an absolute opposite to the narrowly mimetic.

The basic distinctions embody a perennial point of view, one certainly present in aspects of Romanticism and its descendants. When one writer on German expressionism defines its purpose he speaks of the expressionist as one who 'does not reproduce, but creates' an 'expressive deformation which is a personal reconstruction of reality'; he stylizes, tends to caricature, black humour, the grotesque; he seeks the 'absolute' creation of 'imaginative subjectivity'. The perennial necessity is to find terms which characterize the rôle of the imagination in literature and convey the total opposition to the tradition of the copyist of 'the world as it really is'. The recent domination of the novel with its paraphernalia of mimetic slogans, the implied contrast with the poetic doctrines of Mallarmé (still present in Sartre) of poetry as a thing apart, has created a quite intelligible desire to find — or at least refind — a critical terminology for imaginative prose, and has consequently discovered at least one of its crucial concepts in myth.

But what is the 'myth' that the imaginative novelist 'initiates'? It is hard to isolate any clear notion of this. The usual ways of describing anti-mimetic fiction are either to point to certain specializations in the use of language that are highly stylized and non-naturalistic, or to the use of fantasy. Neither helps us much, and it is hard to escape the conclusion that myth remains a story, but a story somehow more freely conceived, with 'myth' merely standing for whatever freedom from the mimetic the particular case implies. Here 'myth' stands for the gap between the literal world of naming things and the uncreated world. But this gap by its very nature is irreducible to the literal and whatever term may be used for it draws its strength from its unanalysability.

I have already remarked that the effectiveness of the particular myth depends upon, among other things, literary criteria. Put this way it might seem to beg the question, and what is important is the way in which the myth acts within the work as a whole. It would be tempting to try to discover the rule by which certain myths may seem to exercise a greater spell than others, but to say so would be to say it in terms of ourselves, to confess that it is some conflict within

WILLIAM WOODS COLLEGE LIBRARY

55476

our own civilization that has given to the Oedipus story some pre-eminent claim on our imagination. A psychology of myth-makers would be required to describe the relationship of inner need and chosen form.

Yet the range of mythical sensibility in modern literature hardly suggests the predominance of a particular model. In choosing the inevitably alien the modern writer is often eclectic or syncretic, through the very act of choice referring to the pressures of his own situation. And many modern versions of the classical myth, say Antigone or Theseus, are not exactly simplified models so much as a frame on which to construct an intense and immediate story, which uses its classical source more for its narrative shape than for any particular meaning the myth might be thought to have had. Gide's *Oedipe* or *Thésée*, or his use of the Philoctetes story as a parable of the artist, are essays in remaining within the form that the myth has established, yet turning one's literary heritage to the service of the immediate. One might say that Gide had kept the story and discarded the myth. For Racine Thésée was the eternal figure of jealous authority confronted by unintelligible revolt; for Gide he is a modern intellectual analysing his own identity. Of course it is obvious enough that whatever mythological device an author employs he still belongs to his own age. Yet there is a curious transparency which seems consciously employed, a gathering of echoes which accompanies the imposition of a form to which the sense of the mythic evocation lends far more than the 'chosen' story. In this whole process the rôle of choice, imposed by his own situation on the contemporary writer, is difficult to separate from less easily formulated motives. Whatever depth and intensity derives from the adoption of a myth is mingled with a distancing which renders conflict accessible to form.

It would of course be easy enough to give an extended

account of particular purposes which can be glimpsed through the employment by a modern writer of any particular mythical element in his work. What excites a particular imagination may be incalculable and what is said about it may be misleading. There is a remark of Camus's about 'the world in which I am most at ease: Greek myth'. Clearly the individual sensibility may find its *rapport* with something remote or alien and find in myth, or some variety of myth, an imaginative liberation. That differing forms of myth should appeal to individual modern writers might lead to the insistence that it is a form of sensibility which is as various as the individuals who share it.

The belief that through myth one touches upon primitive energies, captures elements of the unconscious and sub-rational qualities of the human situation, mingles strangely with the antiquity of inherited form. The search for a cure of souls that might point to the requirement of a distinctive and definable level of belief mingles with the vague – yet irreducibly full – echoes that follow on the patterning out of mythical allusion. And for some writers – say, Eliot – these functions fade imperceptibly into each other. This fusion, perhaps at a variety of levels of consciousness, may be elusive, but its very existence is important. For the emphasis on the element of choice, of artificiality, of eclecticism – all obvious enough in the modern writer's use of myth – might falsely suggest a form of weakness in its reliance on the derivation. The complex relationship of the mythical elements when a writer brings the whole of his literary and intellectual heritage to the working out of his own moment is hardly conscious in the thin and calculating sense of the word. So when Eliot found his interpreters made too much of certain allusions and not enough of others, he was of course acting as his own interpreter, and was perhaps no more open than they to the richness and variety of what had once worked its way into his poem, or when he described *The Waste Land* as mere 'rhythmical grumbling' the deflation is clearly directed against decades of critical interpretation, a gesture of self-defence against the freedom of the reader. And when Forster turned his back on the lurid ink spilled over the Marabar caves to say 'It was just that in India two and two didn't quite make four' he kept the interpreters at bay by replacing one opacity with another.

2

Myth and interpretation

The use of mythical patterns, divine presences, the discovery
of underlying structures of ritual origin, the assimilation of
particular literary works to universal archetypes, have all
become the commonplaces of modern critical practice. The
reasons for this, and the problems which underlie such
critical procedures will best appear, I think, through a
series of cases in which myth is used as an interpretative
device. I shall begin with the simplest kind of case, where
correlations are made between an aspect of plot or character and its mythical prototype, with the intention of
finding a new dimension or level of meaning in the particular work. I shall go on to more complex cases, and
finally to the overall relating of literary genres and mythical
patterns in the work of Northrop Frye.

1 Mrs Bennet and Mrs Ramsay

Consider the following passages:

The once pretty Mrs Bennet, whose sole concern is to get
her daughters married, is an embodiment of the
unthinking life force that works through women. . . .
Her motherhood and earthy mentality might at first
suggest identification with the Earth goddess, but an

explicit clue indicates she is the goddess of love, born of the sea – she is a native of Maryton, the town of *mare*, the sea.

If Mrs Ramsay resembles Rhea, she appears almost an incarnation of Demeter. This divine being, the Goddess of the Corn, was the daughter of Cronos and Rhea and the sister of Zeus. But unlike him and the other Olympians, she was, with Dionysus, mankind's best friend. Hers was the divine power which made the earth fruitful. . . . Symbols of fruitfulness cluster about Mrs Ramsay. She plants flowers and sees that they are tended. The others, thinking of her, associate flowers with her immediately. She adorns herself with a green shawl. . . .

Now the latter passage is part of a straightforward, literally intended, analysis of *To the Lighthouse*; the other is from Douglas Bush's well known parody 'Jane Austen and the Dark Gods'. Aside from any question of the facetiousness of tone which might distinguish the parodic from the high serious, how are we to determine the validity of the identifications, or decide whether or not one of these 'works' as interpretation while the other does not? There are several issues here: at the most literal level, have the gods in question been correctly identified? Do the critic's correlations between divinity and character make sense? And without asking at this point what sort of 'sense' this would be, there are perhaps two levels upon which one might investigate: has the critic found the right clues? And, does the overall sense of correlation somehow seem right, in that all of its aspects roughly cohere?

In so far as the clues are concerned, how do we distinguish the intentional inanity of Maryton, from the case of Mrs Ramsay and the green shawl? After all, green can be associated with other characteristics than fruitfulness – Heinrich Zimmer sees it as the colour of corpses in his treatment of the Green Knight. And flowers might well have multiple affinities. The tests one may apply to the 'clue in itself' are partly those of 'seeing a resemblance'; something quite indecisive when seen in isolation if only because resemblances may be so difficult to pin down, and any one example may suggest many resemblances. And they are partly those of deciding that some isolatable word, name, or image is significant in a way that goes beyond what we might normally expect from its context. Multiple clues may lead to more than one identification and so to multiple mythical personae. This does not worry the present student of Mrs Ramsay: she not only incarnates Demeter and resembles Rhea, but Persephone as well. Mr Ramsay is both Zeus and Cronos. And while the desirability of using some of the clues seems questionable – 'Whereas Rhea has six children, three boys and three girls, Mrs Ramsay has eight, four boys and four girls' – the assumption has been quite reasonably made that whatever symbolism Virginia Woolf employed was not rigidly schematized but worked suggestively through a series of unsystematic hints. However, this glimmer of common sense, rather than leading away from the literal identification of gods and characters has led to a multiplication of them. Not only might we find many of the clues absurd, but the possibility of the coherence of varied aspects is obscured by the multiple identities. I have, for example, omitted the Oedipal aspect of the matter 'which is so clear as to be almost unmistakable', and where the complex family relationships might throw up some justification. Virginia Woolf's known interest in psychoanalysis might give some support to this latter claim, although there is no serious effort to distinguish the author's conscious use of such overtones from the perhaps less intended associations ascribed to miscellaneous deities. Two senses of 'getting the right clues' should be separated: the one involving some intentional connection, the other more like seeing a resemblance. And with the latter almost any word we use to say that it is a relevant, interesting, important, useful, etc. resemblance, raises further questions of justification.

For this particular critic the further difficulties do not seem very important. There are no worries over what competition among clues might imply, or whether or not one clue may point in a multiplicity of directions. He almost operates a principle of 'the more gods the more light'. And behind this may lurk the libertarian attitude that any resemblance that may strike us is somehow relevant – a view that might even validate Mrs Bennet as the goddess of love. Yet if we are to relate the 'clue' to criteria of relevance of any kind it is important to ask what is meant by 'resemblance' or 'similarity'. If one sees no connection whatever between a character and its mythical correlate it is perhaps possible to point to a very rough sort of stopping place. After all, there must be some divinities that Mrs Ramsay does not resemble. Yet such a stopping place is not much help in deciding whether or not flowers and green shawls have some Demeterish aspect which goes beyond the most ordinary sort of middle-aged lady who potters about the garden and has the usual British taste for ghastly green.

The critic's temptations of course do not proceed from what is ordinary but from what is not. There is no doubt that Mrs Ramsay is a remarkable woman, or that a number of devices are used to single out, not only the more directly observable features of her character but those more elusive aspects which she somehow controls. Like Forster's Mrs Wilcox, her 'presence' both informs the character of a place, and transforms the quality of the human events, thoughts, feelings, that exist in a particular atmosphere she has so largely created. What help are the mythical associations proposed by the critic in isolating and describing these elusive qualities? And does this question make more sense if one moves away from the particular 'clues' to the larger resemblances of which the clues are supposedly a part?

I shall return to these problems of evaluation, but it is important to see that the implicit claim of these mythical resemblances is to a kind of 'aspect-seeing' which is part of the larger problem of comparison and analogy which runs through all forms of the criticism of the arts. So much of what seems impressionistic or arbitrary is so in the sense that one is always claiming with comparisons: 'Don't you see it?', 'It looks like that doesn't it?'. If one says 'No' the specific aspects being compared must be described in other ways to bring out the alleged similarity. If the reply is 'Yes, but why?' one hopes to claim that the answer is that somehow the comparison brings out either the essential bones of the thing, or some exciting feature or aspect that would otherwise be overlooked. It is a form of revealing or bringing into focus. If we ask what makes an aspect 'essential' or 'exciting', we are asking about a particular case rather than what might be essential in comparison in general. For the features that concern us are not factors in the working of comparison, something for which no general rules would seem to be useful. 'Comparison' itself may only be said to exist through the observed particular.

But the use of the mythical comparison implies a slightly different kind of force, for the resemblance claimed is not entirely of particular to particular, but of particular to something larger – if not universal, to something that goes beyond a given case in such a way that the particular can be assimilated to a variety of others. Demeter is not a person, nor a character in another novel, but the personification of certain natural powers, and it is toward those powers behind the personification that the comparison is reaching. Also, if one wishes to compare, say Emma Bovary with Anna Karenina, the comparison must work in terms of multiple contexts, provided both within the novel and by the novel's own place in the life and works of its author, and of that life in its own age. But to compare a character in a novel with a mythical figure is to contrast the elaborately controlled with the relatively open, for the figure drawn from myth is subject to none of those localizing restrictions or precise delimitations which apply to the inhabitants of either the living world or works of art. So this variety of 'seeing-as' is relatively controlled at one end and open at the other. This accords with what is often its aim in linking particular and universal: to illuminate the distinct and localized through the more general and abstract. A critic can speak of 'the Tristan formula' which gives a curiously scientific flavour to what is then postulated as a universal 'archetypal' model. The connection may be presumed to work in such a way that the multiple Tristan figures of literary history are somehow seen more clearly through an abstract model which is fundamental to them all.

If, however, we assume that the resemblances are sufficient that we can see some point in the comparison of Mrs Ramsay with Demeter, we might still ask what the comparison adds to our knowledge or understanding – I mean with specific respect to the capacity of the model or 'formula' to illuminate the particular case. To me the example suggests the very feebleness of explanations of this kind. The myth may seem thin and lifeless compared to the density and richness of the work which is supposedly 'explained' by it. What I shall wish to argue is that this type of 'aspect-seeing' is based on a mistaken notion of the rôle of comparison: that the particular is best explained through the more general. And this error has the corollary that the 'meaning' of a work of art is best brought out by pointing to analogous forms that exist on a more abstract level. To talk of meaning in this way is to obscure the more fruitful working of comparison where particular works cast an oblique light upon each other through a complex pattern of similarity and difference, made intelligible by one's sense of how the context works. The move from the particular to the abstract deprives the comparison of that solidity of presence in context, through which the most interesting forms of comparison come to life.

This direction of explanation, moving from the particular aspect to one which has larger claims, brings out what is clearly one of the major motives behind myth criticism. But there is also a related motive, which might be described as 'seeing in depth'. Below the surface of the work in question, it is suggested, lies a deeper level of meaning, and the discovery of the mythic presence points to this level which is perhaps the most important one for the serious reader. Frye speaks of the way in which '. . . the bumps and hollows of the story being told follow the contours of the myth beneath'. And this may also be related to psychoanalytic notions which assume that beneath the conscious world of everyday life lies a deeper world of the unconscious, revealed in dreams, in flashes of mystical insight, and manifested for much of mankind through myth. To see the myth beneath the surface of literature is to plunge more deeply into the human condition, and so to see the very way in which literature intensifies, concentrates, and reveals the human depths.

Again, let us consider this in terms of Mrs Ramsay. Suppose that the points of similarity between Mrs Ramsay and Demeter have been established, that the overall feel of the correspondence is recognized, the personification of fruitfulness is admitted appropriate, to what extent do we feel that our understanding and response have been deepened? Here I think that there is a large degree of subjectivity of response, which depends very much on certain cultural and intellectual features of the critic's own situation. Does he feel that in the very evocation of the past the confrontation with the archaic presence stirs him in some important if perhaps irrational way? The very remoteness and complexity may be moving in itself, and our feeling for the prehistory of an image is a form of historical consciousness that has a special value in a culture that is more and more rapidly cut off from its past. The interpreter needs the myth if the text does not.

Hitherto I have talked as if the work of literature were a fixed point, with an innate and immutable character which the critic then explored, to return with a reading which enables us to see the work more clearly. But of course the process is more reciprocal than this, although the nature of this reciprocity and of its consequences are often happily ignored in critical practice. To write a book is to invoke the possibility of a reader and there is at least some sense in which works change as we involve ourselves in them. The more 'deeply' and sensitively we are committed to what we read, the more intense and demanding the features of an historical moment, the more we are brought to new ways of reading – as the Renaissance came to its allegorical readings out of the conflict of beliefs within itself.

But what degree of involvement does the case of Mrs Ramsay suggest to us? However deep the well of the past there are some trivial dips into it. Some of its evocations may proceed from a technique that is taught rather than something which is authentically felt. How are we to decide which is the case, and what test are we to apply to the notion of 'deeper levels'? There is an uneasy relationship between the 'do you see it?' feature of aspect – seeing and the desire to see somehow beneath the surface, as there is between genuine insight and wishful thinking or academic habit. And the very notion of 'depth' seems to have a vague and suggestive value rather than pointing to anything in particular – the presence of Demeter more a plea than a perception. To say that the myth presents this sense of depth, is to rest upon many assumptions. Perhaps two questions above all should be asked: Is there such a thing as a 'deeper level'? And what would be said about such a deeper level by the invocation of the 'dark gods'?

2 'Mythic significance'

It is in the field of American literature that one finds some of the most remarkable essays in myth criticism. This is partly due to the overtly symbolic or allegorical character of so much American writing. The whiteness of the whale, or the darkness of the forest are open invitations to interpretation of whatever symbolic or mythical kind. So, for one critic, Huckleberry Finn's father Pap 'attains intense symbolic stature in his brief but violent pilgrimage'. This symbolic character is illustrated through the appearance of his face:

> . . . it was white; not like another man's white, but
> white to make the body's flesh crawl – a tree-toad white,
> a fish-belly white.

And the conclusion is drawn that 'there is in this description a supernatural quality that links Pap with Melville's whale'. The 'divine Huck' has sprung out of the 'dark union' between Pap and The River, giving him a 'connection with violence and terror', but which also 'puts him in touch with the deeper human forces which cannot be neatly filed under sociological headings'. His 'connections give him a depth and reality' and he 'transcends the empty rituals of Tom Sawyer's universe and achieves mythic significance'.

The general argument which these phrases are used to embellish does not depart from the conventional reading of the book. Put in somewhat different language it says that the world of Tom Sawyer is one of artificial and childish games conducted within a framework of safety and respectability – hence a level of genuine sensibility and depth of human feeling, a freshness and honesty that the conventionality and fantasy of Tom Sawyer can never provide. Now the difficulty with this rather more deflationary version of this same (or quite similar) reading lies in its very flatness. It could be expanded by a closer analysis of character and situation, yet still make us feel that some mysterious element of the story was omitted by the 'common-sense' version. What means are available to the critic who wishes to capture this mysterious quality? And how are we to regard the notion of 'mythic significance' to which Huck 'attains'?

Take the famous river passage. It is hardly described in language which indicates that it has any supernatural character. And if compared with a more self-conscious kind of description – say the ritualized use of the commonplace in 'Big Two-Hearted River' – it seems quite artless and casual. It is obviously no ordinary river journey, yet it is almost necessary to create the elements of mystery out of the very absence of anything portentous, or any effects other than simplicity and naturalness. Does it then lend itself to the kind of interpretation which holds that 'Having killed himself, Huck is "dead" throughout the entire journey down the river. He is indeed the man without identity who is reborn at almost every river bend, not because he desires a new rôle, but because he must re-create himself to elude the forces closing in on him from every side. The rebirth theme which began with Pap's reform becomes the driving idea behind the entire action'?

The 'rebirth theme' we may take it exists at the level of 'mythic significance', but what does it really tell us beyond what the plot itself provides in the faked death of Huck and his ultimate 're-integration' into the Tom Sawyer world? The former episode is almost too literal a piece of foolery – in the Tom Sawyer vein – and the latter hardly a rebirth acceptable to mythicizers. The possibility of escape from a suffocatingly respectable society into some individual authenticity, however brilliantly suggested in the river passage, is in its formal denial a version of the 'rebirth' theme that fits oddly with any of its traditional mythical forms – as would the notion that it began with Pap's 'reform'. The very vagueness with which any traditional notion drawn from the mythologies of the past is found to fit the terms of the literary examples is a normal feature of myth criticism.

But this haphazard willingness to fit whatever term to whatever case is less important than asking what would be added to the understanding of Huck's river journey by such an explanation. The handling of the 'rebirth theme' seems to indicate that when some form of 'mythic significance' is reached it lies beyond normal human significance. This seems a dubious proposition. One fallacy of the 'deeper level' is that of supposing that somewhere, beyond the normal range of human experience and feeling, lies a special world of the mythic, and literary works may enter into this world even when it is impossible to describe what that level is or to say what its existence implies.

'Mythic' has, in these circumstances, become a value term, with very little beyond a minimum of descriptive content, drawing upon other senses of myth in only the loosest possible way, with its claim to some cognitive content equally loosely staked in 'significance'. A strong degree of approval, a recognition of importance, an attribution of high seriousness – all are implied but hardly explained. And this seems a failure of critical imagination in placing too easy a reliance on 'mythic', where the importance of the term almost seems to come from the uncanny reverence in which it is held, from the myth of 'myth'.

Apparent as the difficulties in this may be, one must also see what temptations lie behind it. There is the obvious romanticism in the reference to those 'deeper human forces which cannot be neatly filed under sociological headings'. This is an intellectual muddle, with its crude contrast between the 'deeper forces' and the straw man of a simple-minded sociology. And if the 'connections' with deeper forces are in question, the primary example, Pap and the White Whale, is made with the sort of idle-minded facility that disregards even a minimal degree of thinking the matter out. 'Whiteness' is the only specific characteristic mentioned that might connect the two, and what the White Whale might stand for and why Pap should have any connection with it whatsoever is not examined in any way. The temptation on this level is that of the pretentious and irrelevant throwaway.

The further temptation, which expresses the felt necessity behind the critic's reach into myth, as well as its limitations, is well put by another writer on American literature in an analysis of Faulkner's 'The Bear': 'If a reading of the story as myth results in suppressions and distortions, as it does, any other reading leaves us unsatisfied.' The reason given for this is that only through such an analysis can one answer a series of fundamental questions – all of them 'why' questions – that are posed by the action of the story itself: Why can Ike or Sam not kill the bear? Why can Boon? Why are Boon and Lion characterized in certain specific ways as they are? And why does Sam Fathers die along with Old Ben? The analysis is complicated and I shall mention only two features of it. One is that the questions posed by the story do seem genuine enough; it is obviously important that Boon kills the bear and not Ike, and it is worth asking why. Secondly, these are not questions that are easily answered in narrative terms, but seem to demand another order of explanation.

The result is to treat the story somewhat as an allegory that works through a schematic arrangement of symbols, and it is clear that through such a narrative arrangement

Faulkner is telling us some things of a general nature – about the wilderness, the South, freedom and slavery, guilt and atonement, initiation and self-knowledge, among others. And without some attempt to account for these things one can hardly be said to be reading the story at all. The dangers for Faulkner's work in the handling of such symbolic schemes become apparent in some of his weaker things, but this does not affect the question of interpretation. Here there is no special area of 'mythic significance' but simply whatever it is that the story signifies, and the interpretation moves by necessity out of what the narrative demands. And this involves the question of intention, inexplicit perhaps but definite, undefinable but present. An intention which will not be seen in a superimposed frame, but where the action is unintelligible without its symbolic overtones, and where pointing to an intention is still seeing it through the text, as much an object of interpretation as the 'text' itself.

This is not the occasion for a study of the complex relations of text, intention and interpretation. Nor am I concerned with what other factors might validate this particular analysis. Here qualities are clearly present that the previous essays have lacked: the feeling for appropriateness in the main examples – whatever intentions may have been present we are quite able on other grounds to distinguish between Old Ben as totem animal and Pap as White Whale – greater care in making comparisons, a sense of proportion about the whole story in relation to its elements, and some modesty about the limits of what he claims. But while these features may distinguish it from the cases that have gone before, the motives behind such a form of explanation retain much in common with those behind 'mythic significance'. 'Our response is not intellectual but emotional. The relatively simple story of the hunting of a wise old bear suggests the mysteries of life, which we feel subconsciously and cannot consider in the rationalistic terms we use to analyse the "how" of ordinary life.' Here again the dismissal of rational props, such as sociological categories, openly states the kind of dualism which underlies so much of myth criticism. Perhaps we can spell out the implications in a series of anthitheses: emotional *vs* intellectual, unconscious *vs* conscious, depth *vs* surface, mystery *vs* clarity. And the larger claim is concomitant that the function of literature is to represent for mankind these important but less approachable dimensions of its existence.

It is easy to say that such dualism represents an over-simplification of the problem it is meant to describe, and that our rational and emotional worlds are hardly so neatly separable. Nor is it clear that 'myth' is the easy and direct pathway to whatever depths such a dualism might postulate. What is evident is the need which is represented in the effort to place literature in the whole economy of man's psychic life. Through myth criticism a certain kind of romantic sensibility has endeavoured to find its voice. In opposition to an empirical, common-sense view of the world – however clumsily such a view may have been misconceived – 'mythic significance' sets out the claim for a world of the imagination which conveys the total possibilities of the human situation.

There are undoubtedly external factors which bear upon this. A desire to find some means of indicating the very unapproachability of literature by a hostile community, absorbed in economic and technological concerns, and consigning literature and the arts, and through them the whole of man's imaginative life, to a marginal and decorative rôle. The motive may be admirable, but one must ask if the means is adequate. How far does the imagination find in the exploration of myth a liberating power acting to redress the balance of an intellectual environment which is structured against it? Is it possible that in such a situation myth criticism is no more than an indication of mingled discomfort and aspiration, and that this form of the search for myth is to be seen principally as a symptom of the anxieties underlying the serious study of literature?

3 The multiple Phèdre

So far I have looked at cases with relatively simple uses of the 'mythic' comparison, where 'aspect-seeing' has been intended to work in terms of the correlation of literary situation and some underlying or at least analogous myth structure, in order to convey a sense of the depth or further dimensions of the text in question. Greater complexity arises when more than one work of art is under consideration, when 'myth' works in more ways than one, when the multiple aspects selected throw light upon each other. In Dorothy Van Ghent's 'Clarissa and Emma as Phèdre' the use of multiple forms of seeing-as is asserted in the title itself. Racine's Phèdre is chosen as the model of a certain kind of conflict, of which Clarissa Harlowe and Emma Bovary are, in terms of their own social contexts, later instances. In Phèdre herself, and in others through her, we see the work-ing of the underlying myth – archaic, sacramental, universal – of the unity of love and death, of the tragic power of eros to defy the conventional world of law and taboo at the cost of ultimate fatality.

Two features of this approach give it its flexibility. One lies in the refusal to see myth as an ultimate term of refer-ence, or ultimate framework of explanation. What one sees working through great works of literature is not simply a dimension suggested by a gesture towards a chthonic presence, but something which can be expressed in intel-lectual terms: 'The great traditional love stories present an ironic antagonism between instinct and society, instinct and law.' Love is an occult power pitted against the

multiplication of taboos present in social institutionaliza-
tion. 'The lovers are sacrificed to their passion, which thus
equates elliptically with the passion for death.' (I shall return
to 'elliptically'.) And while this form of the love-myth may
retain some of the archaic overtones of sacrifice, in Phèdre
the passion is not so much destructive in itself as through
the taboos that surround it. 'The archaic, sacramental significance of the myth gives oblique enforcement to the sense
of the automatism of instinct, its uncontrollable, inde-
pendent working, even though, in the more complex
mythical structure, the centre of significance is no longer
renewal of life through death, but the relationship of individual and group.' So a connection is established between
the primitive content of the myth and the social incarnation of the conflicts which it expresses – and this leads back
directly, if not explicitly, to the Freudian notion of civilization as deriving from the suppression of instinct.

Here the 'love-myth' has simply become a traditional and
repeated form of relation between basic elements of experience. The connection with the ritual death of the god is
hypothetical and perhaps suspect. A psychological explanation of the 'seeing in depth' variety is implicit but vague:
'the centre of mythological significance that is pertinent to
our subject, lies in the underthought of the book [Clarissa]'.
What can this 'underthought' be, and how can it present the
'mythological significance'? The presuppositions seem the
same as those of our previous examples. In the case of
Richardson there is the implication that the underthought
is the real thought, that Richardson's moral identification
with his age was so total and unreflective that the unconscious message is the one of real value, and any larger view
of man's psyche would find the official morality of his
creation narrow and uncomprehending. Of course support
for the 'underthought' is found in the sexual imagery, and
Richardson's lack of self-knowledge in such matters is

notorious. Nevertheless, 'underthought' seems a clumsy expression, with its suggestion of levels, or layers of meaning. Perhaps there are circumstances in which this is a convenient way of articulating the conflicts within a quite various work, as long as there is not the implication that works of art are like layer-cakes or onions where the 'levels of meaning' can be neatly stripped away. This case in fact says something almost suggestive of 'levels of myth', by contrasting the 'puritan myth' overtly used by Richardson with the underlying love-myth: the former clearly a pattern of moral beliefs, the latter a pattern of psychological forces. The word means two different if related things in the two contexts, and when it is used for solar or vegetation myths of a traditional derivation, another if less distinctively functional 'level' may be implied.

The case of Richardson is rather special, for reasons that I have given, and perhaps we can see the working of the myth interpretation more clearly in the case of *Madame Bovary*. Two ways of approach to the text are contrasted, even if they do not exclude each other: 'In the book as a novel of manners, Emma is a fool, herself condemned by foolishness.' But her career locates and gives meaning to the society of death that surrounds her 'at the level of myth, where she is a love goddess'. Two readings are possible, and one gives the story a meaning as the other does not. But the claims for that meaning are put in the context of a vision of the society of the novel as 'a complex of abstractions, bourgeois routines, clichés of thought and action, impotent skills . . .', a society that is dead, having 'overpassed sensuality', and being dead cannot die, as Emma can, through having felt and desired. The 'love goddess' embodies the sensual self, extreme, uncompromising, and altogether doomed.

Some of the means of making this identification may remind us of the case of Mrs Ramsay: Emma is seen as

Aphrodite when her face appears under her bluish veil 'as if she were floating under azure waters' and identifications multiply when at her death she becomes 'the May-queen, Kore, earth daughter, who goes (as in the blind man's song) bending towards the furrow, who is, like the corn, harvested by the scythe'. But such correlations do not carry the whole weight of the argument. The love goddess represents psychological and instinctive forces, 'the automatism of instinct', totally unacceptable to a social norm. Here the talk of myth has become a means of enlarging and intensifying what could perhaps be put in more matter of fact terms, but where the use of the myth as a form at least helps to convey by association the conflict between instinct and convention.

There is a further consequence of this form of contrast *Madame Bovary*. It would have been possible to dissociate between the level of manners and the level of myth in the elements of social analysis from those of the 'mythic' level, implying a double action of surface and depth. But the strength of this essay is that it does the exact opposite, and the mythical level, is not handed as something separate but focuses sharply on the other conflicts. The result is a reading that gives a unity, rather than a peeling off of separate strata. So the claim to a mythical level is not one to the autonomy of a special world of myth, but another mode of describing a common world, of indicating the inadequacy of 'novel of manners' as a framework for interpreting *Madame Bovary*, and suggesting those further aspects which any full understanding of the novel should take into account.

I have mentioned more than once that the vagueness in the use of the term 'myth' often seems calculated, and many of the moves in this essay are qualified by such words as 'obliquely', 'elliptically', to emphasize the indirectness of the way in which implication works in these matters. 'Each notation plays upon the same incommensurables.' But the areas of incommensurability are left to our imagination. This refusal to specify the nature of connections, to work towards any exactness of meaning corresponds with an overall, if unarticulated, view that criticism works as a sequence of isolated, or at best, loosely related insights. Phèdre is treated as an imaginative touchstone rather than as the basis of close comparison. There is a fanciful and arbitrary quality in the interpretation of imagery. Venus 'à sa proie attachée' connects with the vulture imagery of Lheureux, perhaps to the point of sheer invention. (Why a bird of prey rather than another sort of predator?) Only a brilliant passage on clothing works out for a passing moment a tightly constructed series of discriminations. What then is the value of this loose tissue of suggestions and allusions, of obliquities so intensely worked?

Such elusive terms as 'appropriateness' have been used to provide a rather crude test for the relationship of a mythic comparison with the character or situation to which it was meant to apply. But even a successful case of close-fitting of this kind suggests a neatness and comfort that is hardly the aim of the best criticism. The word 'insight' contains some connection of the familiar and the unforeseen, has grasped enough of the sense of the appropriate to recognize that similarity is the ground of comparison, yet that an imaginative leap beyond is required. It is this pressing upon the bounds of the appropriate that makes for the freshness and immediacy in not merely seeing as we have always seen but seeing what has not entirely been seen before. By this I do not mean that the aim of criticism is novelty for its own sake, or that it should be judged in terms of the pseudo-discovery which comes from a false adaptation of scientific models to other forms of academic 'research'. But in so far as works of art are alive and evoke responses or reflections, our interpretative powers will grow through this partial failure of 'smoothness of fit', in which 'appropriateness' has a double aspect. Neither 'seeing-as' too neatly, nor too fantastically, but a mixture that gives life to the particular case by shifting it from habitual ground.

Can there be a saturation point at which the number of aspects seen of a particular work have so multiplied that the 'original' whatever it may be has been wholly lost? This possibility must be considered. Although whether or not the original is blanketed by interpretative dust must depend on its intrinsic qualities. And in the case of 'the multiple Phèdre' there is an immediacy which gives a vividness to the contact of images with each other. The presuppositions may have much in common with the case of Mrs Ramsay, but the final effect does not, and we may wish to elevate a slightly meretricious verbal excitement and intellectual verve over the dullness of academic routine.

One of the issues that has already concerned us is of course raised here as well. The critical practice of seeing by means of myth represents so obviously an historical conditioning of our own, an imaginative insight localized in our own situation, and cutting across those other historical localizings that would isolate *Phèdre* from *Clarissa Harlowe* and *Madame Bovary*. Our own urgencies incline us to an imaginative ruthlessness, of which two extreme versions illustrate the familiar dilemma. One is the fallacy of the inviolable text, the notion that the text is simply and purely there, saying just what the author said. Of course such an hypothesis is a useful corrective to the tedious subjectivities of others, and is perhaps a useful fiction for, say, the editor of a Shakespeare play who may hope to reach something more authentic than the all too obvious quirks, exaggerations and follies of his predecessors. Yet the very palimpsest of glosses must be a constant reminder that the editor himself is the creature of time and that what we see depends upon what we are capable of seeing. That judgments are relative may not, however, deprive us of all confidence. *Lear* as theatre of the absurd may seem genuine in a way that *Lear* as Christian allegory does not. Is there no rule that enables us to balance and evaluate these multiple subjectivities? Experience suggests that as far as myth is concerned we 'see' them less as intrinsically 'there' than as the refracting lens through which our sensibility and its object interact. Our resource must be in some kind of double vision in which 'the multiple Phèdre' is authentic but invented, relevant to its origins, yet our own.

The opposite to the inviolable text is the notion of an inner text or sub-text that must be found beneath the surface of whatever words an author may have chosen to leave us, a text which liberates all of the finder's art. This is purely an assumption which leads to such arrogation of importance on the part of the critic that it can only be justified by an original literature of commentary, the real interest of which has nothing to do with any notion of validity in interpretation. Much of the best in modern French criticism is of this order, engaged in issues which are common to both writer and critic, and using the former as no more than a point of departure. Whether or not we should wish to call this 'literary criticism' is an academic matter. Although myth criticism works so largely on the 'sub-text' or 'underthought' hypothesis, it seems unlikely that such an ultimate separation from the works themselves could become the guarantee of an intelligible autonomy. What kind of autonomy might proceed from a development of a language of myth will be considered in the following section with reference to the work of Northrop Frye. But these cases have drawn their life from the texts they set out to interpret. The obvious intellectual energy and style in 'the multiple Phèdre' do not change this feature of the undertaking. And it is by refusing to make the 'underthought' into a separate imaginative country that a sense of proportion has been preserved, and the substance of that 'underthought' held in view as part of a complex whole.

4 Myth and order

If 'the multiple Phèdre' has represented, in a wholly personal and fragmentary way, the use of myth in the service of the individual *aperçu*, the polar opposite is to be found in Northrop Frye's *Anatomy of Criticism* where myth provides the basis of a literary typology, and hence the foundation for a concept of order in the pursuit of literary studies – an order which in spite of its mythical frame reflects the indigenous structures of literature itself. So much has been written about Frye, and his work has had so great a vogue that I shall limit myself to two quite restricted aspects of his large and varied *oeuvre*: the rôle of myth in the establishing and ordering of literature as a systematic body of knowledge hence providing the ground of interpretation, and the functioning of this mythical sort of ordering in the interpretation of particular literary works.

Frye has assured us, both in the *Anatomy* and elsewhere, that 'the system was there for the sake of the insights it contained; the insights were not there for the sake of the system'. Yet, criticism is 'a systematic study', literature an 'organized body of knowledge', and those who find 'parenthetical insights' in Frye's work are assured that 'the insights could not be there unless the structure were there too.' Also: 'It is clear that criticism cannot be systematic unless there is a quality in literature which enables it to be so, an order of words corresponding to an order of nature in the natural sciences.' Yet this assertion about an 'order of nature' perhaps distorts the idea of a model derived from the natural sciences themselves, creating a misleading notion of what kind of coherence or unity a scientific body of knowledge may possess. For the sciences do not make assumptions about the mystic unity implicit in some 'order of nature'. They only require that scientific laws should not contain contradictions and should not conflict with each other. This is a kind of negative coherence which comes simply from requiring that the bits and pieces which we can explain, among so many others that we can't, have some sort of correspondence.

The problem this search for a coherent order creates for literary study is the subject of a large literature. Here I shall only state the basis of what could be an extended argument. Literature, in so far as it is an intelligible whole, is so by accumulation and continuity, not through any internal logic pertaining to an 'order of words'. The analogy with science as 'a systematic body of knowledge' is so remote as to be unintelligible if taken in any strict sense. What Frye is doing is to suggest in an essentially vague sort of way that the body of the world's literature is a whole which can be examined as such, and any comparison used to enforce this suggestion is to be taken utterly metaphorically. Which is perhaps the only way it could be taken. He gives to his 'systematic body of knowledge' as an 'order of words' no limits and no defining characteristics which distinguish it from other orders of words. And whether or not it is what Frye would wish, this is exactly as it ought to be for the employment of myth as a principle of order. In fact, what we have in the *Anatomy* is a mythical structure devised for the explication of other mythical structures, bounded and defined by mythical limits. All, in a sense, is as it should be.

I shall consider the consequences of this by examining two kinds of use of mythical explanation: that of the cycle myths to show the defining characteristics of comedy, and the use of the archetype drawn from myth to interpret a particular play. Perhaps it is best to begin with the largest-scale use of such a scheme – the identification of the four seasons with the modes comedy, romance, tragedy and satire. It is worth noting that the rather broad and flexible use of the term 'myth' that one has had to employ does not correspond to Frye's own usage. For him the word 'myth' is at least theoretically restricted to a rather traditional type of narrative, while he employs 'mythos' to describe some of the wider sense which we have come to use. However, this distinction is not consistently held and Frye often uses 'myth' in a quite free modern sense. The notion of mythos may involve the wider senses of narrative, which Frye classifies as: literal, descriptive, formal, archetypal and anagogic. Or it may be narrowed to the four archetypal narratives: comic, romantic, tragic and ironic. I do not wish to become involved with Frye's classification schemes as these often involve the highly personal insistence on a series of definitions which may make a kind of formal sense in terms of each other, but are less clear when taken out of their context. The very use of 'mythos' as narrative 'considered as' allows for the widest range of interest in narrative of any kind. Hence what looks like a rigid scheme, working very precisely in its own frame of reference, is seen at every point to open out in such a way as to obliterate precise uses or fine discriminations. Normally for Frye a classifying system is introduced in order to give certain rough points of the compass, then the points are obscured by turning the categories into mixed ones:

> ... when we examine fiction from the point of view of
> form, we can see four chief strands binding it together,
> novel, confession, anatomy and romance. The six
> possible combinations of these forms all exist, and we
> have shown how the novel has combined with each of
> the other three.

What follows is a description of how the strands combine or fail to combine in a number of particular works.

Whether or not generic names add to the understanding

of the works they describe, in my principal case it is merely that the identification of the four mythoi – spring with comedy, summer with romance, autumn with tragedy, winter with irony and satire – are far from one-for-one equivalents. In the case of our mythoi: 'comedy blends insensibly into satire at one extreme and into romance at the other; romance may be comic or tragic; tragic extends from high romance to bitter and ironic realism.'

The degree of stretch and internal variety implicit in all of this can be shown easily when Frye sets out what is the 'total mythos of comedy', which has

> what in music is called a ternary form: the hero's society
> rebels against the society of the senex and triumphs,
> but the hero's society is a Saturnalia, a reversal of social
> standards which recalls a golden age in the past. . . . This
> ternary action is, ritually, like a contest of summer and
> winter in which winter occupies the middle action;
> psychologically, it is like the removal of a neurosis or
> blocking point and the restoration of an unbroken current
> of energy and memory.

This is an attempt to give a schematic description of the overall pattern into which comic action may be seen to fit. The oddity lies in the fragmentary character and curious isolation of every element introduced in explanation. 'Ternary form' is no more than mentioned, and its musical uses untouched. The seasons enter in passing as the participants in a ritual contest. The section is preceded by a discussion of devices in comic plot and followed by one on the types of comic character, which in turn is followed by remarks on the social grounds of comedy. Observations of a variety of kinds are made, with profuse examples, but their relationship with the schematism is hardly worked out.

The problems of the schematism are shown by the comparison of the six phases of the comic mythos with the analogous phases characterizing romance. For comedy: 1 the ironic in which the hero is in jeopardy, 2 the quixotic where the hero merely escapes, 3 the revolt of youth against the senex, 4 Arcadian romantic comedy of the green world, 5 the pensive romantic, 6 the esoteric retreat. I suppose that it is not an objection that the demarcation lines are sufficiently awkward that one feels the fit of example to category seems pre-arranged in favour of the latter. Nor perhaps does it matter that for some phases the examples seem somewhat specialized, as in the single case of À Rebours for the sixth phase. What matters more is that the criteria for the definition of the phases differ considerably from one to another. Some are distinguished by the relational elements of plot, others by character type, others, perhaps especially the fifth by a quality of tone, others such as the sixth by such special psychological criteria as 'oracular solemnity' (or is this tone?) and the desire to return to the womb.

The development of romance is quite different. The six phases 'form a cyclical sequence in a romantic hero's life' and can be represented as a life story: 1 mysterious birth, 2 innocent youth, 3 undertaking of the quest. Yet with 4 we have a vision of the happy society, in 5 the moral stratification in a detached and contemplative view of society, while 6 contains the movement from active to contemplative adventure. Somewhat surprisingly: 'Collections of tales based on the symposium device like the Decameron belong here.' In this sequence the opening is based on the cycle of life while the second part turns to images of the human situation based on varying degrees of detachment in its appraisal. And in one case at least, this detachment in the sixth phase is determined by the mere existence of a narrative device. So when comedy and romance are compared there are further variables in the order of phases. The principles that determine them are, in fact, neither consistent within a series nor are the two series developed in an analogous way. Nor is the outer frame of the four seasons invoked to much purpose. Frye's own imagination often seems to be making a series of doubtfully connected moves, based reasonably enough on affinity, resemblance, and degrees of resemblance, or sometimes on opposition: youth and age, light and dark, etc. That these are capable, with the four seasons and the ages of man, of endless permutations should not be surprising, and a theory of myths as a principle of order is only the loosest sort of packaging.

The clearest, if not the most sympathetic, effort to give Frye's use of myth a reasonable order is Wimsatt's account of the steps involved in the underlying conceptual scheme of Frye's work, in which myth is the metaphorical and analogic embodiment of man's 'assimilative wishes' – that is, the accommodation of himself to the alien natural order by an act of imagining (which is not unlike its mediating rôle for Lévi-Strauss). 'There is one basic and inclusive myth which takes the shape of a divine quest, death and rebirth, following the cycle of the four seasons.' Perhaps such a hypothesis would give an overall unity to Frye's work, although I have often thought that its greatest interest lies in the varying distances and tensions between what it says and what it presupposes. The underlying monomyth as a fundamental form on which endless literary variations may be played, suggests a tidiness that is alien. The ordering of the various literary kinds seems to rely very little on a fundamental mythical model. And whatever hints of such a monomyth there may be are points of reference which may be evoked at will, or suggestions that convey a deeply felt belief in the unity of literature, rather than an actual mapping of the relations between the multiple forms of the imaginative accommodation.

There remains the question of Frye's use of myth in the interpretation of particular works. It is not easy to approach this through the *Anatomy* where interpretation is often limited to the reference that places a literary work in some large category. But the relationship of genre and the seasonal cycle reappears in *A Natural Perspective*. Comedy 'is based on the second half of the great cycle, moving from death to rebirth, decadence to renewal, winter to spring, darkness to a new dawn'. And the cyclical scheme is applied to *The Winter's Tale*, the 'winter's tale' of violence and storm being followed by the second dramatic action: 'an action of irresistibly pushing life, heralded by Autolycus's song of the daffodils, and growing to a climax in the great sheep-shearing festival scene, where the power of life in nature over the whole years is symbolized by a dance of twelve satyrs. The reviving force pushes on . . .' bringing with it the obvious plot resolution. It is puzzling to ask oneself how helpful this has been. It is perhaps Frye above all that Graham Hough has in mind when he says: 'In its application to any particular literary case myth criticism turns out to be curiously disappointing. It tells much of interest, but not what we really want to know.' Granted that we may want to know different things of different texts, and different things at different times of the same text, there is something strangely evanescent in what we get from Frye's criticism. Take his remarks on the effects of what he calls the 'archaizing tendencies' in Shakespeare, which 'establish contact with a universal and world-wide dramatic tradition'. We are introduced to a 'kinship' that connects *Pericles* and *Cymbeline* with *Sakuntala*, *The Winter's Tale* with *Epitripontes*. And the link with myth and folk-tale is such that 'we may say with some confidence that if archaeologists ever discover a flourishing drama in Minoan or Mayan culture, it may not have plays like *King Lear* or *The Alchemist*, but it will have plays like *Pericles*'.

Of course there are two presuppositions here that give substance to the uses of the myth. One of them – whether true or false – is that character has ceased to matter, that we do not care about Leontes as we care about Lear, but about the cycle of the story. What matters in *Pericles* is dangers averted, and an ultimate rediscovery – nothing in particular about Marina or Pericles. The strange joy of the lost found, of identity (whatever identity) rediscovered, of the 'story' successfully completed is somehow a different joy from that of private feeling, or that proceeds from any complexity of the inner life. And a joy that has been felt to dwarf the latter in its simplicity and radiance. I shall want to return to the consequences of this in thinking of the differences between the 'myth story' and the 'real story'. For the second pre-supposition is that the 'myth story' means more than the real story – and more in some deeper, simpler, if intangible, way. That by setting it beside the complex and 'real' the myth is charged with a revealing sort of sense. Yet this does mean a view of the working of the myths themselves. The story of Persephone is a story, yet seems nature rational-ized. Other stories are more opaque, and do not hand one something that works so schematically.

The force of the 'archaizing tendencies', the sense of their reach into the immemorial past, nevertheless rests on a historical fantasy. Delightful in a way, but hardly bearing much weight. And Frye's treatment of *The Winter's Tale* is based on a simple polarity in which the more general re-marks have an attraction – even if through their splendid arbitrariness:

All myths have two poles, one personal, whether divine or human, and one natural: Neptune and the sea, Apollo and the sun. When the world of sea and sun is thought of as an order of nature, this polarization becomes a god or magician who controls the natural machine at one end, and the natural machine itself at the other. Tragedy, irony, and realism see the human condition from inside the machine of nature; comedy and romance tend to look for a person concealed in the mechanical chess player.

And this delight in general formulae is in the end handled with a deferential tentativeness before the text:

> The normal action of a comedy moves from irrational
> law to festivity, which symbolizes a movement from one
> form of reality to another. The world of tyranny and
> irrational law is a world where what is real is given us
> arbitrarily as a datum, something we must accept or
> something of this in *The Winter's Tale*. . . .
> reality, the reality we see to be 'out there'. The world of
> the final festival is a world where reality is what is
> created by human desire, as the arts are created. There is
> something of this in *The Winter's Tale*. . . .

The real world which is reached through the play 'has none of the customary qualities of reality. It is the world symbolized by nature's power of renewal; it is the world we want; it is the world we hope our gods would want for us if they were worth worshipping.' But as an old tale, a mere fiction, what it leaves us with is 'neither an object of knowledge or belief'. Here, it seems, our involvement is with Frye's own vision of comedy, and of art itself: 'The world we are looking at in the conclusion of *The Winter's Tale* is not so much an object of belief as an imaginative model of desire.' This vision may appeal through its own eloquence, yet lead us away from the *The Winter's Tale* towards what we may seek in the play. And the movement of mind is away from interpretation towards the interpreter himself.

There is an analogy to Frye's cycle of the seasons in the use of the four elements in the work of Gaston Bachelard. This is an attempt to provide a phenomenology of the poetic imagination through the way in which poetic imagery coalesces around the poles of earth, air, fire and water.

Through an associative method which borrows from psychoanalysis yet adheres to no rigid psychoanalytic theory Bachelard pursues the possibility of the combination of images. The emphasis on the primacy of dream, of the unconscious realizing itself through a reverie which may reach poetic form, produces a rich and varied series of critical remarks. This is primarily a study of the categories of the imagination, based on the presupposition that the imagination participates in the world through unconscious affinities with its material elements. This approach is intentionally oblique and should be judged in terms of its indirect account of the imaginative process, not by its illumination of the particular literary text. Yet the continuous reliance upon example, the play of one set of associations upon another, the intricate weaving of the concrete and its imaginative consequences – all make one ask how far literary explanation may demand a fuller account of the imagination's working. Not perhaps in the sense of a 'theory', but of an extended description of our forms of the ordering of experience, of the quasi-conscious patterns which gather around certain 'magnetic' poles of our thought.

The relation of this type of investigation to the study of myth may be hypothetical, but the use of the concept as an organizing principle is clearly an effort to give shape to similar a-logical patterns and affinities. 'In myth', says Frye, 'we see the structural principles of literature isolated.' Yet if structural principles are to be seen through myth, the order it produces is quite different from the introduction of categories – a-logical rather than logical, contained in a narrative and imaginative form rather than in conceptually related divisions and sub-divisions. And to express the working of myth in conceptual forms is to risk the contradiction of other assumptions.

In some senses Frye seems to oscillate between the use of

a categorical scheme and an association-based series of connections which can only roughly be related to categories. Of course this is a rough distinction in itself, but it may help one express what seems an underlying difficulty for Frye as well as defining one or two characteristic problems of the Bachelardian exploration of imagination. Both Frye and Bachelard seem to rely on what might be implicit in 'natural' association. Indeed, it would be difficult to associate spring with death or renewal with autumn except in the terms of some highly specialized context. And just as certain associations of the four seasons are too natural to ignore, the elements of earth, air, fire and water have, partly through accumulated tradition, partly through an equally natural series of associated images, their own kind of magnetic pull – showing affinities and connections through irregular but distinguishable patterns.

How can we accept as 'explanation' those loose groupings of images and allusions that represent the mind's escape from the world of logic and practical consequence? To what extent are such patterns an acceptable form of order in the study of literature? They at least seem modest when compared with the energy which goes into Frye's macro-schematics. But even such a word as 'schematic' may be subjected to figurative use, and in the case of Frye we have seen that no element in any one schema is related in any rigorous way to any other, that the schema is simply a means of assembling multiple kinds (and degrees) of similarity; it provides a thread through the labyrinth rather than a well-ordered set of pigeon-holes. This may not of course wholly exhaust the possibilities of myth as a source of shape for the imagination's workings, but the tension between the schematizing impulse and the freedom of intellectual play which Frye's comparisons reveal, offers nothing in the way of an ordering procedure which others might find useful. The explanatory force of the general category is too slight, or too obliquely applicable to the particular case. If we look for the illumination of the particular it comes in the intermittent fragments of contact, of passing and impressionistic touches, where the meeting point of two works has its individual moment, ancillary perhaps to some intended service to the larger category.

Again, this indicates a kind of criticism that turns away from the traditional Anglo-Saxon commitment to interpretation. It has been an almost unchallenged presupposition of our critical thought that criticism is some sort of second-order language which comments on, explicates, or explains something quite distinct from itself: a literary work which is assumed to be an imaginative creation of the first order. Frye violates this presupposition in two important ways. First, in spite of individual insights of the greatest interest he is hardly concerned, especially in the *Anatomy*, with particular literary works and their interpretation. He almost reverses the process by using literary works as examples, or even as 'explanations', in his own mythic scheme. So 'the opening rose-garden episode of "Burnt Norton" gives an extraordinarily complete summary of the symbols of the analogy of innocence.' It is the analogy of innocence that is in question, not what to make of 'Burnt Norton'. The literary work acts as the 'explanation' of a symbolic scheme, making the critical work the first-order language on which the example acts as a commentary. I do not know to what extent Frye intends it, but this is the usual way in which the examples relate to the working of the whole. Second, his lack of concern with particular literary works, and breadth of concern with literature as a whole have created his own intensely personal form of metacritical language, perhaps of a third order, working at a higher level of abstraction than we normally expect of critical talk:

Just as the organizing ideas of romance are chastity and

magic, so the organizing ideas of the high mimetic area
seem to be love and form. And as the field of romantic
images may be called an analogy of innocence, so the
field of high mimetic imagery may be called an *analogy
of nature and reason*.

Here everything is directed to the largest views of literature,
in which a particular work and its characteristics could only
have a subordinate rôle.

An effect of these two factors is that the 'third order' and
the 'first order' tend to conjoin. The structure of the metacritical 'argument' is imaginative: it exists, and quite
intentionally as the title of the *Anatomy* indicates, as a
creative work in its own right, exercising Wilde's paradox
that at its highest level criticism is more creative than
literature itself. The assumption of such a 'first order' rôle
is of course not unique. I have already mentioned that the
aim of much modern French criticism in its revolt against
Lansonism is not to understand or interpret the literary
work but to use it. To use it as the point of departure for
commentary which is not recognizably a critical task, or
second-order task, but which addresses itself directly to the
human situation. The text, the point of departure, is simply a
means, the utterance itself like the 'literary' one which preceded it, a form of *écriture* – a concept which obliterates
the simple stratification of 'orders' which our more usual
critical presuppositions may have relied upon.

But if one imagines that, as his construction evolved away
from any more conventional notion of interpretation, Frye
was creating a model which others might follow, this would
be a serious misapprehension. For one of the most marked
features of the *Anatomy* is its inward-lookingness, its strong
sense of privacy, of belonging to an individual and sometimes eccentric imaginative world. On a smaller scale something like this was true of 'the multiple Phèdre', where a

deeply personal excitement in certain images created from their varied literary incarnations an intense, oblique and revealing series of connections. Yet there too we were led away from any of the narrower and more conventional meanings of interpretation, to concentrate on certain energies, obsessions and themes from which a vivid and controlled language has created its own kind of unity.

Judging by the creative criteria that it sets for itself the *Anatomy* may pose a self-destructive standard, and be seen as one of the curiosities of what 'the age demanded', a remarkable if eccentric episode in literary history. Certainly it has not marked a new stage in the development of myth criticism, but seems the last, and greatest, monument of a genre already well in decline, where in spite of the inwardness of vision the genuine intellectual energies are startlingly centrifugal, contained only by the profound perversity of invention reaching out for its own art form.

5 The decay of the mythical comparison

The early cases in this chapter, however crude and mechanical, yet raise matters of importance for our consideration of the rôle of myth in interpretation. For they pose in a straightforward way the question of what sort of interpretation the 'translation' of particular literary works into their mythical equivalents may achieve. Or to put it in another way, if we assume that all of the mythical correspondences, ritual repetitions, archetypal figures and relationships have been discovered and defined, what does the existence of the myth beneath the surface tell us? How much more do we understand of a work through seeing the presumed skeleton beneath the skin? Does a mythic tale underlying a particular fiction have a meaning that the fiction itself does not? Something must be added, or there would be no point to the exercise. But to describe the new element added by such interpretation as either 'a new dimension', or 'a way of seeing' would have two quite different sets of implications. The presuppositions here are seldom sorted out in critical practice. I have given reasons for thinking that there are difficulties in the notion of myth as a super-added dimension. Although the temptation of 'the story beneath the story' obviously draws its strength from the depth implicit in 'beneath'.

There is a further problem in asking why it is that the myth is assumed to be intelligible in a way that the surface narrative is not. One may believe that the identification of abstract qualities, even in the case of Mrs Ramsay and Demeter, has a conventional kind of explanatory value. But in so far as anything said about Demeter does no more than refer to a story, the use of a story to explain a story violates our habitual convention concerning orders of language, and does not really accord with what we would normally think of as explanation. Even if we suppose that a mythic tale has an acceptable abstract meaning, as we perhaps usually assume the Oedipus story to have one, it is important to recognize the degree to which this meaning is both highly conventionalized, and is distinctively a modern superimposition. Any attempt to attribute literal meaning to Greek myth will be shot through with ambiguity, for the tales are so deeply immersed in their own cultural context that any careful study of them shows their unreliability as a source of intelligible models for any kind of critical purpose. Far from containing any ready intelligibility they are remote, complex, mysterious and opaque. Whatever clear-cut and accessible meaning they have is one that we have invented for them. The ready-reference to the 'Oedipal' element in whatever work is the easy post-Freudian shorthand of which we expect little more than the recognition of certain highly schematized and simplified relations within the family group. That such terms become the easy usage of popular journalists or the capsule analysis of undergraduates has little enough to do with Freud and even less with the tale employed by Sophocles and Seneca. There is a connection no doubt, but the process of dilution and simplification has provided us with something no more than a tag. The difficulty with using the most obvious shorthand in critical language is its lack of interest.

Myth for the ancient world may have expressed a conflict, a contradiction, the impasse of terrible forces. It gave form to the working of fate itself: for Oedipus there is a monstrous necessity, even if worked out in the world of contingent fact – of the mistakes of messengers or the rationalizations of advisers. And for Freud the choice of the Oedipus tale to express a fundamental psychological relationship may have a vitality of a 'second order', yet the mixture of rigour and imagination gives it a far-reaching life. But when this notion too is borrowed and re-used a gradual process of distancing sets in, through which the fundamental energy in the original conflict echoes more and more weakly through succeeding examples.

For the modern mythicizer it may become less the expression of conflict than the evasion of it, a groping for intelligible form in the chaos of the empirical world. And if so, the Oedipus myth has merely become a formula, useful as a means of casual identification, with any of a number of degrees of looseness or precision, of the rough outlines of a psychic phenomenon. The stages represented here may follow our conventions of orders of language easily enough, presumably moving towards some kind of abstraction where the assumption of ready intelligibility may be justified in that their terms have been assimilated into a more abstract language – say, that of psychoanalysis. Or is it rather that such comparisons simply show a ready-made resemblance, a pre-digested form of 'seeing-as' which tells us no more than how comparisons fit into conventional expectations? Here again, only the particular case gives ground for any judgment. However the assumption of intelligibility may be one of those expectations which obviates the necessity of saying anything more about the matter – as in the 'Oedipal element' in Mrs Ramsay's family life.

Could we devise rules for the effective rather than the conventional uses of the mythical comparison – or a schematism for representing the degree of decay present in any range of uses of a particular comparison? I can see little use in such an undertaking. For one thing it is subordinated to the larger matter of the death of myth (which I shall consider in Chapter 3); for another, we may well applaud in terms of economy and precision, or even for the effects of ironical inversion, what lies very far from any primary insight.

Or the sudden presence of myth in the narrative may be strangely catalytic, as when Proust speaks of Swann searching through the cafés and streets of Paris like an Orpheus in search of his lost Eurydice. The simile transforms the city itself into a vast kingdom of the dead: Swann the man of art in pursuit of his living object lost in and to the world of death, with the implication of second and ultimate loss – and irony in the realization of what Odette is really up to. The effect of the image is a total shifting of the reader's angle of vision, a darkening and intensifying of a private pain – far different from the critic's simplifying model it is a dramatic device for throwing an inner dimension of love's anguish into startling relief. It is not the story of Orpheus, nor the presumptive 'meaning' such a story might have, but the wider implications of the underworld search, concentrated in a phrase.

The myth here has a rôle, in one respect at least, analogous to the simplifying use of the model narrative, which is implicit economy – of bringing many things together, of suggesting much through little. Yet here the use is so literal and intentional as to have only the slightest resemblance to the more hypothetical 'seeing' of the myth form beneath the real and phenomenal surface. But I have already given reasons why this latter is a notion with only the most limited possible uses. The story with the meaning 'built in' presupposes either the conventional or traditional accumulation of what is to be the story's accepted sense or, as with the case of Persephone, that the implicit rationalization is an obvious one – ready made for derivative use.

The temptation remains to say that whatever meaning for the real story is derived from the 'built in' meaning of the myth is in some way more abstract, thinner, less alive than the world a vivid fiction portrays for us, as if we were, in seeking any mythical dimension, trading a rich and important thing for its shadowy simulacrum. Cases like Mrs Bennet and Mrs Ramsay would convince us that this is true if it were not unfair to judge a method by its weaker examples. The case of 'The Bear' was of course different in involving a large if not wholly determinable degree of intentionalism, and part of the strength of that analysis lay in its bringing out the degree to which Faulkner's narrative had drawn upon certain traditions without itself looking thin and artificial. And to say of the long hunting passages that some kind of initiation is implied, that the *rite de passage* is an underlying part of the story, is partly a matter of convenience, a sort of synopsis, again a kind of conventional labelling which uses terms susceptible of a quick and accurate understanding. Such a shorthand is justified by the wide acceptance of certain terms – their ready availability as explanation, without any necessary claim to exhausting the subject. The impoverishing effect is found largely in the more mechanical and forced use. The 'forcing' of the mythical dimensions in 'the multiple Phèdre' was somehow a capturing of a special quality of critical insight, rather than a reasonable accounting for what one could properly expect to be there. And there may indeed have been a time when the *rite de passage* in 'The Bear' came as a surprise – as it still must do to generations of first-year university students. In such a case the built-in 'meaning', consciously planted by the author, stands in a perfectly easy relationship with the story. Yet we feel the encroaching danger of an excessive tidiness, a readiness to tie up the richness and complexity of things in a neat well-labelled package.

The mythical comparison then puts a double face upon what 'the age demanded'. At one level it may seem a curious form of setting out the inner meaning of literary works that enables the critic to 'find' something, to say 'here is the meaning' and to represent the myth beneath the skin with the ease of a taught and transmittable technique. But far more important is what it tells of the nature of literary study for the better part of a generation of scholars and critics. I have approached this through the problem of interpretation, and one can see through the prevalence of an interpretative method the very notion of what literature itself might be. Yet if literature itself can only come to life through the mythical beings that sprout in its 'sub-text' it either says something about the artificiality of literary teaching – its mixture of hot-house atmosphere and intellectual ineptitude – or about the extremity of the need to find degrees of relevance which go beyond any traditional place literature might reasonably claim in giving us a sense of ourselves, our world and our destinies.

Both levels of what 'the age demanded' may be simultaneously true, with artifice and urgency mingled. And the moribund specimens of the mythical comparison have represented the transformation of urgency into formula – the natural evolution of any original source of intellectual energy through the workings of large institutions. It would create too easy a target to dwell too much on the effects of institutionalizing a form of study. But it is important that what is transmitted is not merely a 'method' but a series of preoccupations, a commonly held if not totally articulated recognition. So if Frye's 'system' has seemed inward looking it has had a public analogue in the very system of university teaching of which it is so much a part.

In speaking of Frye as a last incarnation of such an institutionalized 'mythical movement' one certainly has no desire to denigrate what is surely its richest and most creative example. Yet the very self-enclosedness of Frye's 'system', the fragmentary nature of the critical rewards in the best of myth criticism, the crudity and banality of what is not the best, might seem to override whatever original moment of imaginative excitement myth may have once provided for the interpreter of literature. Or perhaps it is rather that such excitement has its value beyond interpretation in the analogies between myth and literature, in the way in which the existence of myth provides the intellectual and imaginative possibility of a 'language' in which the analysis of the human condition may find a freedom and range impossible to more logically responsible conceptual languages, yet which has an intelligibility, a sense of 'relevant', 'applicable', 'usable' meanings which lie this side of 'poetry' itself.

3

The myth of myth

1 *The necessity of fictions*

We have been dealing, not always explicitly, with the
relationship of two concepts: story and myth. There is one
sense in which the general notion of 'fiction' embraces both,
and in much that has been said it has been implicit that a
theory of myth is, for any literary consideration, a theory
of fictions. Therefore it is worth considering the degree to
which we think of myth as a compelling or somehow
superior fiction from which a kind of acceptable or at least
usable frame of reference can be devised, if not for the
understanding of life as a whole, for the pursuit of particular
ends. And such particular ends, of course, constitute their
own set of claims on 'life as a whole'. How coherent do we
expect our lives to be? How deeply do we expect the parts
to be consonant with each other? How full an explanation
do we wish of the rationale of any such consonance?

Take the degree of overlap in 'story', 'fiction' and 'myth'.
In a story something happens, whether it is a relation of
what actually occurred or what might have occurred. And I
have spoken on several occasions about the way story so
permeates the myth that it is impossible to separate from it.
But it is obvious enough that many stories are not myths,
while the 'myth of' locution (some of which will be seen

in the next section) manages to use the term without anything more than a distant gesture towards a narrative content.

Stories may be in many degrees true or false; they may organize events, impressions, perceptions to create an order, with that order depending on the specifically sequential type of connection that we associate with narrative. It is a more general sense of the constructed and intelligible which informs theories of 'fiction'. Certainly of the three terms 'fiction' implies the highest level of generality, while 'story' the lowest common denominator of narrative content, and 'myth' a rather consequential and specialized extension of both terms.

If one were to set out the conditions to be filled by a general theory of fictions it would embrace far more than the literary sense of the term, and the very generality of the concept would create the essential problem. For one thing it is related to a wide range of philosophical views about the function of language, and its relation to human life and social structure. These views could be set out in roughly the following order:

1 Our knowledge of the world is contained in and conveyed through language.
2 Whatever form of enquiry we undertake it is language which is primary and not the world which it describes – because we see things through it, it determines the nature of what we see. We may change the nature of our categories, our ways of organizing what we do with language, but we cannot escape it or the fact of seeing by means of it.
3 And some draw this further consequence: any view of the world is therefore inevitably false in the absolute sense. What we can do is construct intellectual means to serve our language, time and culture-bound purposes, which will have a partial and relative validity in so far as they may be tested

by the natural social circumstances to which they are applied.

4 Hence scientific hypotheses, logical and mathematical meta-languages, the explanations of historians, the concepts of Freudian psychology, the descriptions of novelists are all 'fictions', constructions of the human intellect and imagination which we may put to the particular purposes for which they were designed. The various fictions proceed from different methods and aims and that they are not intelligible in terms of each other is something we should take for granted. There is no total view of the world as an intelligible whole, and it is our fictions that we shore against our ruins.

I do not of course mean that any one philosopher or philosophical school holds precisely such a view, and it is put in sufficiently rough form that it might accommodate quite a large variety of opinion. Nor is this the place to submit any element in such a picture to philosophical scrutiny. My aim is only to point out the range of the concept and the variety of its implications. Certainly the use of the term 'fiction' to cover such a multiplicity of functions does not imply that there is any unity in their purpose, nor that we need confuse one kind of fiction with another. The classification systems of South American Indians described in *La Pensée sauvage* may be fictions as Linnean classification or Aristotelian categories are – useful for some purposes and not for others. And while such examples of 'la science du concret' may be connected with their myths they are distinguishable from them. If Lévi-Strauss wishes to define certain characteristics of 'mythical thought' it is through both contrast and connection with other forms of language, of which it is a part.

The implications of such a general theory of the fictional character of intellectual constructs are innumerable, and here I am only concerned with two of them: one is the relation of the literary sort of fiction to others of a quite different sort; the second is the relationship between literary fictions and myth. Both involve the question of the degree to which anything, from scientific hypothesis to historical commentary to the contents of either myth or fictional creation may be considered 'explanatory'. One may, I suppose, take for granted the explanatory features of the more scientific type of 'fiction' on the ground that if they didn't explain there would be no point to them at all. And we are not concerned with the difference between true science and such fancies as alchemy, however much it may have crossing points with the world of myth, because essentially both claim to unfold a series of causal relationships, and present a working hypothesis with practical consequences. Yet the transposition of alchemy into the imaginative world of *The Magic Mountain* gives it a different function altogether – a source of psychological and imaginative order, rather than gold from sand. While not wishing to draw a distinction between scientific and literary fictions, because both are imaginative in the fullest sense, it is important that the one requires the fulfilment of an exact series of expectations while the other may imply with variable degrees of exactness. One may ask of both the second law of thermodynamics and of *Anna Karenina* if they are true, and know that one means the question in totally different ways. In such matters the conventions that govern explanation are appropriate enough and usually sufficient to make clear the character of explanation required.

With the case of the relationship of myths and fictions the former is obviously a subdivision of the latter but this does not give any automatic solution to the problem of what quality of expectation or explanation may be forthcoming. How do we assess the fictional? Frank Kermode has suggested what amounts to terms of structure. In *The Sense of an Ending* he works out a terminology of completeness, of the nature of the relationships among parts, of the stages of beginning, middle and end. The terms 'consonance' and 'concord' stand for the successful resolution of the multiple elements into what must have some acceptable and satisfying symmetry. There seem to be two defining characteristics of the fiction itself: that it involves sequence, that is, time sequence, and that such sequence be 'organized'. 'Plot' is defined as 'an organization that humanizes time by giving it form'. The 'escape from chronicity' characteristic of fiction lies in the artist's power to recreate and rearrange, to force time's submission to the concords that inner necessity requires.

Kermode tries to make a clear-cut distinction between a fiction and a myth, partly on the ground of the level of credibility they claim. 'Fictions can degenerate into myths whenever they are not consciously held to be fictive.' The difficulty with 'consciously held' is in the number of questions that it begs. Myth is held to claim a totality of adequate explanation, to call for absolute assent (and oddly, to belong to the order of time lost, as fictions to the here and now). Anti-semitism is a myth and *King Lear* a fiction. Dark as the implications of both may be, the one has the ugliness of a false ground for action, the other is only a vision of despair. Between the gas-chamber and the call for a looking-glass there is the absolute difference of assent to a form of monstrous action, and imaginative assent to the monstrous contingency of things. The effect is to make 'myth' so wholly consequential, in the literal sense, and fiction so wholly inconsequential that either of two queries are inescapable. If consequence is the criterion of the myth, the reasoning becomes circular in that the fact of consequence makes the distinction. And if the 'fiction' is marked by the acceptance of its unreality, why take any 'fiction' to heart at all? Of course we know that after the film or during the novel the tears are real, the situations are 'real' enough. The child's question is never wholly answered by saying 'it was only a story'. For in the latter sense two events may to us be identical: the life of Beatrice Cenci, and the dramatic poem based upon it.

Furthermore, Kermode has not sorted out the relationships of past and future, in that, by his own reasoning, the dangers of myths may lie in their power over action even if this may depend on the formulaic grip of the past. Of course anti-semitism may lead to action, and *Lear* will not, although dramatic 'fictions' have been put to such a purpose, as in the performance of *Richard II* on the eve of the Essex conspiracy. The understanding of the conspirators must have been painfully limited to a narrow view of a work which most of us would see quite otherwise. Its character as 'call to action' and as work of dramatic art seem alien to each other. But such use raises exactly the issue of what it is to believe in a story or the possibilities a story may open up even when a fiction does not pretend to be anything else. What comes out of the Kermode distinction is something like this: fictions are in some sense 'explanatory', yet not the bases for action. They have no literal claims on our belief, yet they die if they cease to make the sort of sense that helps us make our own worlds intelligible. They do not require the falsifiable premise of validity in action.

So what appears as one level of contradiction in Kermode, that fictions are 'explanatory' yet not to be believed, is repeated in another fashion by his concept of myth. In his view it seems to claim something further than being 'believable' but has become in some sense 'believed in', in such a way that myths may be the sources of misconceived action. What Kermode has not clearly sorted out is the relation of the way in which a belief is held to the content of that belief – erroneous or otherwise. So a notion of myth based on the way in which a belief is held gives no criterion of the truth or falsehood of any such belief, of its efficacy or lack of it in explanation, or of its social desirability. He has at the best given us a persuasive definition. For most purposes, the difference between 'being believable' and being 'believed in' may itself express a gradation, which still falls short of absolute assent. Just as the sense of an intelligible story may move in any number of degrees towards some kind of useful explanation.

The arguments over the 'explanatory' character of myth have in traditional anthropological studies centred on the way in which the myth has provided some account of the framework of life: birth, marriage customs, laws, the animal kingdom, the cycle of the seasons, and death. This of course means myth in the traditional and 'prescientific' sense. And if we are in some sense in a new age of myth it has been clear that it cannot explain in such literal terms. Although Maritain sees the force of myth in its relation to belief: 'the metaphysical myths are the organic signs and symbols of a faith actively lived', and 'such myths have no force except for the faith man has in them'. Against this we must put Kermode's interest in the way in which books, the fictions modern men have made, arrange the events of human life into intelligible relationships: 'in the structure of time, in the concords books arrange between beginning middle and end', concords which are 'consolatory' for reasons impossible to specify but which enable us to feel 'the imagination's mercies'. Kermode's concern with time is to measure our sense of 'perpetual crisis' against 'the long perspectives'. But consolation is ambiguous, especially if easily won, and 'Those [books] that continue to interest us move through time to an end, an end we must sense if we can never know it; they live in change, until, which is never, *as* and *is* are one'. This is a rather impressionistic passage, but the uncertainties it is grappling with contrast forcefully enough with the either/or literalism of Maritain.

An analogous description of the problem is that of Alan

Watts which distinguishes between 'enduring' and 'explaining'. Science and philosophy 'explain' the world to man (although one might suppose that these might be rather different sorts of explanation) while religion and art, the fundamental mythmakers, enable him to 'endure'. But what consolations support such endurance is difficult to say when the clear implication is that the ground of such consolation is in direct conflict with whatever it is that science and philosophy have explained. The bases being different would seem to imply that the one was false and the other true, although this is clearly not the author's intention. The feeling is not very distant that 'enduring' involves a kind of fatalism that is tempered by the occasional fairy tale. And the tendency to face the dark conclusion in so much of modern literature may be partly the turning of one's back on the possibility of the consolatory concord. Indeed, the ordinary solace may be to much of modern sensibility profoundly offensive, and the delight in disorder or in primal energy may inform certain aspects of the myths that we find most dear. Or is it another form of consolation to like one's reality plain? Certainly the modern demands upon myth have shown, along with the shaping possibility, a taste for the violent. And these may exist in no particular relationship but simply as alternative aspects of our sensibility. To see some symbiotic pattern or form of reciprocity would be to invent the hypothetical psychology of the modern mind.

It is with extreme situations, ultimate questions, particularly with the question of death, that the 'sense' of the ending seems uncertain help. Although this is a case where Lévi-Strauss emphasizes the mediating (if self-contradictory) function of myth, and Jung calls on the need for myth to explain where reason can tell us nothing, to give 'helpful and enriching pictures' which are neither right nor wrong, but where the 'archetype follows the tracks of life and lives right into . . . death'. It is easy to accuse such talk of some calculated areas of vagueness. How one sees right through into death seems sheer assertion of a function one could not possibly explain, which by the very nature of its language falls short of the literal. What is important is to attempt some evalution of the way such pictures work and in what way mythic understanding is in any way useful, in the human situation towards which it is directed. Certain situations may call for a certain type of 'picture' with exactly the right level of ambiguity built into it.

The notion that myth is something apart and subject to special rules is already present in Frederick Schlegel: 'Mythology has a great advantage. What at other times flees from consciousness is nevertheless to be seen here and held fast in a spiritual sensuality.' Two things may be seen in this, woolly as the terms of it may be. One is the realization that Schlegel was seeking a form of understanding which captured those elements of experience that were otherwise evanescent, elusive, not easily captured by logical or empirical forms of knowledge. The other is the sense of the concreteness of form in which an understanding would be conveyed. 'Spiritual sensuality' may be unintelligible on the surface of it and to suggest some of the fancier terms of German thought. Yet it conveys the conjunction of concreteness and implication.

So I shall suggest that what the myth does is to present a concrete possibility. To our openness in the face of ultimate questions to which we have no answers and for which explanations are simply not explanatory the myth poses another question 'It's like this, isn't it?' And what follows is a story. A story which we may call a 'myth' in the more traditional sense of what the gods did and what men owe them for it. Or a story in the sense of a 'fiction' in Kermode's wide use of the term. The story proves nothing. Yet it has a certain force. If we can be seen to say to ourselves – even in the crudest form – 'Yes, life's like that' or to feel that the human sequence of things is somehow illuminated or made intelligible in a way it was not before, the story has somehow worked.

'Somehow' – in every phrase I use, the tentative and speculative nature of what is being said is all too obvious – and as freely admitted. The story is simply there, and the connections between it and its supposed implications to be seen as possibilities, caught in the imaginative leap in comparison or analogy. No answers ready? But what kind of questions are they? The very tentativeness of reaching for the story, of asking, 'will it do?' may imply that there are also certain questions to which literal answers are not appropriate and that there may exist an appropriateness of another kind. 'What can be asked can be answered.' But these are in fact questions which if so asked are not to be answered for they are not really asked. Hence a blur in the *Tractatus'* line between the logical and the mystical. We are concerned here with a form of discourse which is neither logical nor mystical, which is part of the human situation but not in any strict sense of presenting an argument or of conveying empirical knowledge.

And we cannot dismiss these 'questions' because their logical oddity forces them out of habitual categories. You can't ask certain things about human character, nature, destiny etc. and get literal answers which make literal sense. The choice between no answers at all and answers of an oblique and tentative kind keeps the ambiguities of evaluation before us. But at least in all of its tentativeness – 'is this what it's like' – the thing that the myth provides is a recognizable thing, which is more exactly related to the question in hand than a more abstract and logically responsible answer would be.

But why not common-sense answers? And by this I mean the sort of empirical observation that we normally make about human affairs in their ordinary sense. Both the scope and character of these 'ultimate' questions are not usually answered in such terms, for they are subject to social conditioning of all kinds, and the criteria of acceptability are created by such conditioning. But the experience of modern literature has acted to cast doubt on the remark of Renan that 'the myth really possesses its full significance only in those epochs when man still believes himself to be living in a divine world'. Indeed, as he perhaps could not have foreseen, the very opposite is the case, and it is only through the disappearance of a divine world that myth has come into its own.

In trying to characterize the shadowy but distinct possibilities of a 'third language' that 'makes sense' which is neither logical nor empirical, one keeps returning to the motives, the energies, the felt needs which lie behind the postulation of such a language, rather than the precise form which it might take. And if we return to our earlier definitions of myth, it is the vaguest among them that serves our purposes best: that of 'a schema of the imagination' which is 'capable of organizing our way of viewing the world' (Joseph Margolis). But this capacity for 'organizing' has two features: first, an indistinctness as to the character of a 'schema' which might allow it to 'organize' in a variety of quite different and unspecified ways. Second is an ambiguity not merely as to the content of the 'schema' but as to the level of claim which such an 'organizing' would effectively make. Such an organization of our view of the world requires some explanation of how fully we accept such an arrangement, an understanding of what kind of acceptance is implied – of how we are moved, shaped, consciously perhaps involved in an acceptance, and yet may not in the end literally believe. For the importance of myth in a 'demythologized' age, is not simply to provide us with the now missing sense of an ultimate frame of reference, but to provide an area of almost deliberate uncertainty as to what such frames might possibly imply. And the strength and weakness in myth reside in the same thing: the weakness in the fact that we can always ask 'what is meant by this?' and the strength in some level of conviction that this is not really a relevant query to whatever it may be that the myth 'says'.

But what kind of knowledge is it which says 'I know that that is what it is like', 'the image fits', or otherwise fails to do so? Or further, what if one feels that it is something that a fiction shows that makes the difference between a world in some sense ordered and intelligible, and one in which the parts don't fit, the whole thing falling into disordered fragments? This is of course a contrast that novelists themselves have understood and explored. No one more than Proust on the occasion at the end of his first volume when the narrator walks in the Bois de Boulogne – a garden, among other things, in the 'mythological sense of the word'. The change in the course of time has altered the spectacle which he once remembered in terms of the aesthetic harmonies of an earlier fashion, into one which is no longer coherent to his eye.

And to all of these new elements in the spectacle before me, I had no longer the faith to bring which would give them consistency, unity, existence; they drifted loosely in front of me, haphazardly, without truth, containing in themselves no beauty which my eyes could have tried, as they used, to see as an intelligible whole. . . . But when a belief disappears, there survives it and with increasing vividness, to mask the lack of the power which has deserted us of bringing reality to the new, a superstitious attachment to the old things which belief had animated; as though it were in them and not in ourselves that the divine is present, and as if our actual failure of belief had a contingent cause – the death of the Gods.

And as the narrator's final discovery is that time can only be regained by a reconstruction of his own, and a world becomes intelligible in so far as our intellectual or artistic powers enable us to reshape it, the divinity is within ourselves as we lift our pen, or brush, or open mouths to shape the sentence. And much of the self-conscious search for myth seems like the superstitious attachment, giving too much of itself to the 'contingent cause', a nostalgia for precisely the quality of explanation which can no longer be given. It is at this point that the myth of myth enters into its own. The power of the artist's shaping may have become the power of the gods, and in any case fully as necessary. That the myth can be shaped, that the 'consistency' and 'unity' can be found, makes the finder his own creator.

2 Myths and their powers

If the last section has attempted to describe the ambiguity of the modern demands upon myth, I should now like to set out more fully the areas in which this ambiguity operates, in order to show some of the necessities which are working through it and to enable us to compare features of what is implied by its multiple forms. Perhaps it is easiest to begin in the rather simple area of what the taste for mythic pattern, present in the examples concerned with interpretation, may tell us about the expectations felt of narrative. They contrast with the sense in which a complex narrative, say that of Proust, assembles through memory and observation a rich and densely populated world. Proust's is the full case of the fiction moving the mixed elements of perception towards intelligibility. The critical examples, where there was a strong sense of the myth beneath the skin, where 'the bumps and hollows of the story being told follow the contours of the myth beneath . . .' (Frye) tend towards models of simplification. This may not be entirely so for Frye himself who holds that as 'literature develops greater variety and independence of expression, these mythical shapes become the conventions that establish the general framework of narratives. Hence the literary convention enables the poet to recapture something of the pure and primitive identity of myth.' Yet the very sense of the 'pure' and 'primitive' conveys the isolating of an essence. The mythical shape cannot help but suggest a contrast with the other and realistic notion of a story in which all sorts of characters and events may co-exist. It suggests rather repetition and a concern with the exact symmetry of design, just as Kermode brings the model of a plot down to the simplest form: the ticking of a clock. '*Tick* is a humble genesis, *tock* a feeble apocalypse.' All time is contained between, and in a form which is infinitely repeatable.

I have already mentioned myth as an alternative to *mimesis*, but then largely on the ground that it tapped alternative sources of creative power. Another difference clearly lies in the predominance of form, when the interest in the mythical pattern or archetypal presence in a narrative lies in the power of synopsis or simplification which such forms suggest. Hence the predominance of outline over the richness or complexity of individual character, or the surface and material features through which a story may work. Hence neither *King Lear* nor the *Alchemist*, but *Pericles*. And better a magic ring than the Russian countryside, or 'a spider people scuttling among hot stones' than the world of 'intricate moral possibilities'.

For so long the model of a Tolstoy novel has been one of the paramount features of our notion of what sort of thing literature was. In Lawrence's essay on the novel its richness and flexibility, the possibility of conveying the whole of life in its infinite variety, of mixing the formal and the solid – its freedom and complexity – all are held up as measures of artistic worth, and of the justification of art itself. Such an ideal has hardly been borne out in the later history of the novel, with a development towards simplification and symbolism – something obvious even in the later work of Lawrence himself. And the agonizing over the fate of the novel is partly a query as to the abandonment of this artistic ideal, or at least an expression of anxiety at its reduced efficacy, as if the decline of an art form indicated a large and unfathomable shift in the character of our inner selves.

This is not of course to say that the mythic element may not be discussed in 'realistic' works of art, nor that appreciation of one form of art excludes another. Yet the preference for the mythic over the moral, for the ritual form over the randomness of everyday life, suggests that the power of myth is at least partly in a concentration that makes an area of imprecise intelligibility. One may see this preference to some extent in the flight from the kind of criticism, or even that consciousness of literature, that talks and thinks about the story and characters in it as if it were one's neighbour in question. Lévi-Strauss speaks of his distaste for the theatre on the grounds that it is too much like straying by accident into someone else's flat – a thing of no interest in itself. But this reflects a particular sense of the theatre in one of its historical phases, the very one against which the Peter Brook production of Seneca's *Oedipus* was directed.

Kermode supposes an historical transition 'from a literature which assumed that it was imitating an order, to a literature which assumes that it has to create an order, unique and self-dependent. . . .' But this order may be of many kinds, and may be instanced in both of our models of the uses of narrative: the Proustian-Tolstoyan bringing into focus of multiple relational elements, and the taste for the simplified pattern as a form of grasping cleanly what are felt to be the 'essential' outlines. Certainly the latter predominates in the vast majority of the invocations of the mythical, and even more markedly so when the need for identifying touches upon the extended uses of 'myth of'. However the two forms may overlap at multiple levels, and there seems to be a sense in which the term 'myth' oscillates between its simplifying uses and open-endedness, from the tidying synoptic effect of formal order to its innate capacity for blurring an accommodation. Yet Kermode's 'historical transition' is related specifically to making order in our consciousness of time, where indeed the mythic structure might claim to occupy a special place.

But take a simplifying form of ordering and then its extensions. A form of synopsis, of a simplified series of relationships finds an enormous range of uses in modern society, and it is worth looking at cases that may be analogous to the literary ones. Begin with the very notion of self-consciousness in the search for identity. In so many ways I am as I see myself. I invent the myth of myself, to impose on my private chaos some intelligible form of order, in terms of whatever combination of circumstances, characteristics, accomplishments, aspirations or fantasies I may think relevant. I choose to see myself as . . . should one say a hard-working barrister – pillar of the law, a suave and powerful politician, an object of sexual fantasy, a man of genius or of tragic cross-purposes. The range is limitless and of course there are degrees in the level or complexity of the construction. One must be able to distinguish the tag from the process it represents, although often the very purpose of the tag is exactly that of short-cutting the more complex description and giving the sense of the self its nutshell. The modern search is for the appropriate means to give the self which can no longer depend upon its inheritance a defining shape, to choose in effect among multiple possibilities the kind of story that seems suitable to either the self one has discovered or the self that one wishes to be. Of course this is not a neat distinction. Such ambiguity of truth and intention may apply from the simplest tag-making to the full elaboration of autobiography. Graham Greene says plainly that the impulse lying behind his autobiography is the same as that of his novels: 'a desire to reduce a chaos of experience to some form of order'. And Jung puts the matter precisely in terms of myth:

> What we are to our inward vision, and what man appears to be *sub specie aeternitatis*, can only be expressed in terms of myth. Myth is more individual and expresses life more precisely than does science. Science works with concepts of averages which are far too general to do justice to the subjective variety of an individual life.

> Thus it is that I have now undertaken ... to tell my personal myth. I can only make direct statements, only 'tell stories'. Whether or not the stories are 'true' is not the problem. The only question is whether what I tell is my fable, *my* truth.

Explaining ourselves to ourselves, drawing the portrait, finding the tag, telling the appropriate story – of course all of these overlap, or are in some senses interchangeable. And there can be at least some degree of reference to primitive custom, when stories involving, say, the totem animal, or another object with a symbolic ancestry, play a part in forming both individual and group identity. Of course for the totemist it is the group that matters. For our own age the sense of a 'myth of ourselves' may strain against the notion of collective and social forms, and it is exactly this that provides the ground for some of the most important modern uses of the concept. The elaboration of this moment of 'strain' will develop some of the rather brief descriptions of the functioning of myth which in Chapter 1 stuck rather closely to elementary definitions. We can now look further at those powers over the self which relate to a wide range

of social life: fashions, manners, loyalties, degrees of affilia-
tion to one's own society or the sub-groups within it,
ideologies and related beliefs. All areas in which myth is
used to relate the individual to the age, areas in which we
may now try to balance some of the senses of function with
those of explanation.

I mention fashion and manners because there is the
obvious sense in which we change ourselves as we change
our clothes, adopt or forget a taught style of life. As we
choose objects, places to live, surround ourselves with or
divest ourselves of selected aspects of an environment we
may, on differing levels of consciousness, play into the hands
of a 'story', self-mesmerizing or self-revealing. Barthes's
Système de la mode articulates the nature of the code underlying the structure of fashion – the choices and changes that
the noting of fashion involves. And his earlier exploitation
of 'myth of' in the image of a negro soldier saluting the
French flag suggests a form of argument based on a feeling
for social comedy, for the absurdity of what is implicit in
any such 'mythic' object. For here person has become object
within an imaginative scheme imposed by an outlook which
Barthes would describe as that of the bourgeois oppressor,
where the world of objects, styles, images and manners
serves the general views and interests of a class.

Two aspects of this are worth considering – one implicit
if not seriously worked out by Barthes, which is a conception
of levels of myth in which the fragments of the mytho-
logized may support each other at differing levels of significance and generality. And from this might follow an
interchangeability of levels, by which one kind of myth
substitutes for another, in either synechdochic or
metonymic substitution, replacing one level myth by
another, or supporting a larger myth of the widest social
consequences through those that operate in a very concrete
and limited way. It is possible then that one may accept the

latter for the former, or accept the latter and forget the former. I shall return to this question of substitution.

The other is the way in which Barthes works out a precise connection between myth and its ideological use: the right has myths as means of oppression; the left is at least largely myth-free. This distinction is worth examining if only because it is an attempt to work out a systematic series of implications, through defining myth in its social function in a given society and moment in time, to give it its own rôle. This is as the linguistic device of a given class. The bourgeois world is one of manufacturers and hungry consumers of the well-cooked images which fix the mind in a state of timeless paralysis. Among such manufactured items are not only the ephemera mentioned in Chapter 1, but all of traditional literature which is defined by a 'voluntary consent to myth'. Opposed to this is a language of production, active rather than passive, designed to transform rather than preserve. This language is free of myth. 'The bourgeoisie dresses itself up as bourgeoisie and in doing so produces myth; the revolution declares itself as revolution and in so doing abolishes myth.' So myth is an essential part of a conservative political stance, and freedom from myth is a preface to action.

Of course Barthes realizes, working from his own definitions, that such a distinction is vulnerable. There may indeed be a sort of myth on the left, but it is 'inessential' and feeble. This dismissal seems special pleading. Or is it possible that Barthes would revise his view in the light of the evolution of a new revolutionary mythology? He is surely correct about the old style of revolutionary folklore, associated with socialist realism, of the heroic production achievements of the tractor brigade, the exploits of the 'Red Detachment of Women', or the personality cults of Soviet leaders. But the current folklore surrounding Che Guevara suggests a less contrived mythicism, and one which links through pop singers and other culture heroes with even the detested Minou Drouet. Of course the content is different: Minou Drouet may be a bad poet whether at eight or eighty and the myth of 'l'Enfance Poète' an inflated bit of silliness, while Guevara may have been a heroic figure who undertook and suffered much. But however used and in whatever cause they are myths of the same order.

Beyond this, and whether they fit the semiological system in a different way is of little importance, lie Marxist versions of the cycle myths, of the inevitability of certain movements of history as courses of evolution within society, surely a myth of the same character as 'the Eternal Return' or 'the Golden Age'. And beyond perhaps lies the myth of Revolution itself, with its curious halo of rightness-in-itself, of unanalysable and uncriticizable sanctity. Here again is a stance that is surrounded by a mind-freezing paraphernalia of slogans, with those elegant variations that keep the notion alive: 'permanent revolution' and 'revolution in the revolution', each striving to avoid that commitment to fixed structures and both social and intellectual forms that might arrest a movement towards perpetual change. What may have begun in passionate argument and empirical study may well end in slogans, and there is no sense that the left is in any way immune from the mythicized intransitive.

Of course Barthes is right in the emphasis placed by the title of his principle essay: 'Le mythe, aujourd'hui'. It is the construction of the present that counts, and the relationships with a given social order. As F. E. Sparshott says, the understanding is widespread, and the scope of its consequences accepted:

... the question of how a nation got where it is in politics or literature demands a global answer, and calls for a single all-embracing narrative. The place where such questions are oftenest asked is the school, and the purpose of answering them to mould the sense of a common national heritage. What is required is therefore a myth, in which the complexity of what took place is reduced to a manageable series of chapters in each of which a single recognizable contribution is made to what the myth holds we now are. A nation that shares no such myth is a nation with no available past and no sense of its present reality.... The myth changes ... our view of ourselves and our problem changes.

As with classes so with nations: the myth is shaped to the needs of the moment, and myth is the voice in which the age speaks to itself.

Sparshott insists on the 'global' character of the story, and I have mentioned the importance of the fitting of parts to whole, or the way in which myth fragments support the whole outlook which they may be seen to represent. Of course in the wide sense of Barthes, there are obvious discontinuities; the 'myth of' any particular cultural fragment does not relate in a rationalized and structured way to a system of beliefs, but constitutes discontinuous fragments loosely related. So when one says (as in Chapter 1), 'All societies rest on myths' it does not mean a precise series of rationalizations – as Sparshott put it, '. . . the articulation need not be on a single scheme or even internally coherent'. But there are degrees of coherence. If the 'global' myth is not a clearly organized series of conceptually ordered parts, in some sense it 'adds up'. So the bits and pieces produced by bourgeois society may all of them suggest the values held by that society as a whole – its motor cars, entertainments, forms of property, foodstuffs and sex-goddesses relating in a variety of ways to a form of life. If in the Barthian sense the story is in the object it is easily told.

Could one assume from this that there is an enormous supply of fragments, of images, of discrete elements, of mythemes if one likes, out of which larger structures may be devised? It is hard to see this in terms of structured pieces that have a place according to that structure in an even more highly structured 'story' at a more complex and, if not more abstract level, one with more general implications. And it would be difficult to see a large structure built of the appropriate stages without considering the intentions that gave them life. The distinguishing of mythemic fragments makes no sense without something to which one relates them.

At another level or articulation it may be again equally elastic, with the myth of free enterprise, or of learning from the peasants and workers having as many and ambiguous forms as circumstances may require. The alternative stories may create no sense of conflict. Lévi-Strauss discovered among South American tribes that quite different versions of a myth did not seem contradictory, but that the variant was simply accepted in the spirit of 'it may have been like that too'. The divergent, if related, pictures could co-exist. And this may depend on the degree to which we feel that we must put our beliefs in a rational order and conceptual form. My thesis has been that it is the power of providing looser yet imaginatively viable forms of coherence that is the precise characteristic of what we have chosen to call myth.

It has been claimed that certain patterns of myth, both in terms of rudimentary mytheme and of the connections between them which occur in a variety of cultures, often widely separated in space and time, therefore suggest a universal reservoir of mythical forms – or put more modestly, that the stories we tell to make what we think an appropriate kind of sense of ourselves and our situation have a startling degree of similarity. One need not think in Jungian terms. Lévi-Strauss has said that 'a myth is still felt as a myth by a reader anywhere in the world'. It is the story, not the style. This makes it the opposite of poetry, the untranslatable, therefore the most culture-bound of the arts. However the meaning of myth lies not in the elements but the way in which they are combined. It is the structure that counts. And the assumption seems to be that some combinations of elements are universal, even when their claims transcend the framework devised by any particular cultural situation from which it took its shape. This is, of course, one of those points at which more traditional concepts of myth touch on the more modern and looser ones – especially those of the 'myth of' variety. Yet what seems a constant is not any particular structural feature in the combination of forms, but the sense-making function. Different stories do for different moments, whether derived from one's fancies concerning the social value of expensive objects or beliefs about the jaguar and the making of fire.

A curious test of the universality of the sense of certain story forms is that put by an anthropologist working in West Africa, who after listening to a number of tribal stories (which in this context I take to be identical with myths) was required to tell one of her own. Through familiarity she chose the story of Hamlet. The interest in the event was that the narration, as far as it was story, made perfect sense to her listeners, but a sense which is alien to our own. Claudius was the hero – of course one's duty was to marry one's deceased brother's wife. Hamlet was deeply at fault in not having the proper advice of the wise on the subject of apparitions. There are other amusing details: Polonius remains the great fool some critics have seen in him – even if the reasons are not precisely the same. But the question is, if the story was intelligible, was it the same story? One hesitates to say that the story the African elders understood was the same as the one which generations of English school-children struggle to interpret. For the latter there may be problems, but the framework of possibilities is limited. For the former the framework is dissolved in their own cultural presuppositions. That objects, animals, etc., have the same sort of total cultural implications that the equivalents may have in our own, goes without saying. The arrowhead may be as mythicized as Barthes finds the DS 19. But the one is hardly translatable into the other.

The ambiguities in all of these comparisons may make them insubstantial, but the suggestion is very strong that there is such a cultural adaptability of the 'fonction fabulatrice' that the sense of a universal language of myth, or Jungian residuum of eternal forms is less vivid than the sense of a continuum of transformations, through which cultural presuppositions remain the determining factor. Kirk's comparative analysis of Mesopotamian myth finds its basis in continuity of ground. The formal similarities to other stories may tell us that the constants of heaven and earth, of man on earth, in the underworld, or placed among the stars, are repeated fixed poles of the imagination. Yet as the imagination works on its surroundings, its transforming powers may turn to whatever mythemic elements are there before it, from the starry sky to the animal world, the vegetable features of the forest to the canyons of urban landscape and the objects which inhabit them. The Great Bear or the Jaguar, or Brigitte Bardot, or a manufactured object can be an obvious feature of one's natural and cultural surroundings and by some intensifying act of the imagination attain that special state of vague but marked significance where they have entered more vividly into the image we have of our world.

The difference in their power need not depend on whether or not they have entered into a narrative, but simply on their articulation. If myths are sought by a particular culture or age, they are also the product of that age, and if myth, in its expansive sense, is the voice in which the age speaks to itself, then it speaks in many accents. Take a description of them drawn from Robbe-Grillet:

As I cast my eye over a miscellany of scandals and crimes, as I look at the shop windows and advertisements which make up the surface of every great city, when I take a stroll through the tunnels of the metro, I am assailed by a multitude of signs which taken together constitute the mythology of the world in which I live, something like the collective unconscious of society....

It is perhaps this passive, culturally dependent 'collective unconscious' more than the reservoir of forms that creates the most powerful of the modern senses of myth, at the level at which its imaginative claims may both threaten and satisfy.

There are situations in which the many voices may have the surface appearance of existing on the same level: the widely held and working myth of racial equality, and the fake myths invented to serve an end like the Nazi myths of Aryan racial superiority. Yet what is most incredible in Nazism is that any of its irrational farrago could have been believed. Perhaps in fact it was not, yet it became a terrifying social force. On the other hand some of our most dearly held beliefs may rest on no more evidence yet be impossible to criticize. It is not the competition among such congeries which suggest existence at a similar level that is as interesting as the comparison of the hold myths may have when obviously operating at quite different levels. I have referred to the 'invariable weightings' of the term in common usage; the extension of this is in the degree to which different levels of myth may come to substitute for each other. It is this painful awareness of the possibility of substitution of levels that informs the response of a traditional moralist (Nicola Chiaromonte):

Today, instead of the cult of ideologies we seem to have adopted a cult of the automobile, television and machine-made prosperity in general. But this cult is based on a belief fomented by bad faith, the belief that material (industrial technological and scientific) advances go hand in hand with spiritual progress; or, to be more precise, that the one cannot be distinguished from the other, and that the only problem left to be solved is the correction of a few remaining flaws and the removal of some lingering injustice. In plain words, it is generally thought that the production of increasingly prodigious and increasingly complicated 'useful' objects is a good in itself, that is, an absolute. And even if this were not so, there is the underlying feeling that one cannot do otherwise – that one cannot run counter to history. To doubt this is considered simply foolish. It cannot be denied, however, that even while people accept this myth and let it govern their lives, a certain feeling of uneasiness persists and notions like 'alienation', the 'absurd', 'anguish' and other unpleasant states of mind have begun to be discussed. As for those who object to the ideas underlying the myth, they are condemned in the name of 'modernity', 'science' and 'reality'.

The bad faith and nihilism of the modern world is nothing other than acceptance of the empty form of what was once authentic belief in the absence of other beliefs that can be whole-heartedly embraced. This means that one really believes in nothing and lets oneself be swept along by the fatal undertow of events. It is not only economics, technology and politics that are affected by this continual movement but states of sensibility and the life of the mind, so that culture becomes part of a deadly automatic search for novelty, itself nothing more than marking time in the general disorder. In short, the prevailing myth of our time is the idea that the exploitation of all available natural and technological resources and their use for the satisfaction of men's material needs must lead to the general good, and the creation of the best of all possible worlds.

This is in fact one of the two responses that Robbe-Grillet suggests we can make in the face of these modern myths: to condemn them in the name of a higher reality. The difficulty of course lies in the authority such a reality might have, and Chiaromonte's essay has its source in the failure of one such authority: international socialism with all of its humane, progressive, melioristic intentions. The rest is gesture. Robbe-Grillet's alternative is to accept the mythology that the world presents us and to 'play' with it. The artist's re-arrangement is the subordination of such mythological matter to the game he wishes it to play – thus, his myth. As maker of games he is also the maker of a kind of order. The validity of fictions is, as we have seen, not in what they say but in their very existence, in the order-making power. It is not finding *the* order but *an* order: the myth does not stand for anything, but simply *is* something. Does this mean that the mythemic fragments with which the author plays are – like West's 'plasmatic assortment' – the quite arbitrary constructions which in making their own 'order' submit to no rules except those of a particular imaginative choice? Alas, any reader has an external frame of reference, and the game of which the assortment consists cannot escape habitual rules and associations. The avant-garde is defined by what it revolts against.

One may ask of course whether there is any point at all in considering the relations between the mythic fragments of which Robbe-Grillet is speaking and the more global sense of myth which is heavy with belief of a total kind, even less their relation to the inherited sense of meaningful (if not sacred) tale. Or one may ask again whether or not the elasticity of the term has become such that the strength has deprived the term 'myth' of any ground for its identity. This problem, which was raised at an earlier point, can now be given a more decisive answer. The usefulness of the term is inversely related to the precision with which it is em-

ployed – or at least has become so. It is this very characteristic which gives force to what I have called 'the myth of
myth', and three major consequences, at least, are worth
considering.

One is obvious from the remarks of Chiaromonte: the
ease with which the concept allows for the desired – or
rather necessary – transitions from great to small, from
grand beliefs, loyalties, etc. to the small change which may
be substituted for them. And the term 'myth' somehow
makes this series of transitions and substitutions seem
natural. It his given Chiaromonte the convenient way of
expressing his conviction that the process of degeneration
of levels and qualities of belief, and with them of the distinction of the human enterprise, can be expressed as a
sequence, a malign progression, where the levels in question
have the appropriate links. Here the elasticity represents the
conceptual necessity that responds perfectly to a situation.
Perfectly? It might be held that 'myth' is only a term of
convenience which masks the essential features of the
problems in question. Yet I think the process described is so
established as one of the clichés of cultural transformation,
that there would be every reason that a language adapted to
it should emerge.

Second, the very stretch of the concept shows a develop-
ing degree, if not of abstraction, of – again – substitution, in
which the myth of myth works at a different level from
particular myths (of whatever global or trivial kind). And
through this perhaps one can see some law of a paradoxical
nature, that – for the present age at least – the meta-myth,
that is the myth which feeds off its components, attains
some special sense of its own power. This is a form of transformation which – as in the case of Renan's remark about
myth and the age of faith – could not have been predicted
from the earlier history of myth, and underlines the fashion
in which the term has adapted to 'the present age'. For in a

sense it reverses the conventional sense of the imagination's rôle – that is, 'the more imagined the more false' has become 'the more shaped the more relevant'. So Blake's doctrine of the primacy of the imagination has found a modern form, if not perhaps one he would have chosen.

Therefore, to push the paradox, the life of myth is dependent on the death of individual myths, and its power is inversely proportional to the claims that particular myths may employ. We may not 'believe' in the Hanged Man or the Fisher King or the Lady of Situations, but we may believe in the 'assortment' of which they are a part. We may believe not in the Age of Gold, but in Stavrogin's dream of it. And it is the very function of literature – at least for the present age – to establish the claims of this meta-order without demanding any concurrence in the stuff of which it may be made. It was out of the death of Christianity that Eliot created his own order, his own myth. And his subsequent artistic failure lay in taking it too far. The literal claims and clumsy satire of *The Rock*, or the more embarrassingly didactic passages in the *Four Quartets* indicate the point at which the 'myth' has departed, and the ideological preacher is driving the – less acceptable because more literal – message home.

This perhaps expresses the supreme capability of literature, or the effective ambiguity which is inseparable from the nature of a 'fiction'. The myth of myth is the artist's licence, at least in a situation where his subservience to other functions, defined by a less anxious and more exigent social order, is replaced by a total freedom to 'play' or construct. Of course such freedom contains exigencies of another sort. The order that is one's own must be unique, personal and yet intelligible. The assortment must provide a shape that persuades without spelling out. The 'myth' which works through literary means is not so much susceptible to the analysis of its structural affinity with other myths, but a free construction whose very imaginative identity lies in the power to elude. Elude at least the literalism that destroys *The Rock*. Gide was partly mistaken in saying that 'good sentiments make bad literature'. Any sentiments will do. And myth suggests, as the Boyg to Peer Gynt, that the path 'round about' is for us the only one possible, when the content of large sentiments chokes both the possibility of belief and violates the fastidiousness of any honourable sensibility.

Finally, there is the curious reciprocity between the writer on myth and his subject matter, which seems to have as one of its aims exactly this avoidance of too literal a series of claims. To good criticism this comes naturally enough, and I have already mentioned the sense in which Frye's work is a 'mythological' structure. Kermode's making sense of the way others make sense involves a kind of protective (and commonsensical) distancing. And Barthes speaks of his book *Le Degré zéro de l'écriture as* 'only a mythology of literary language'. Lévi-Strauss goes further in his description of *Mythologiques* when he says that 'in seeking to imitate the spontaneous movement of mythological thought, this essay . . . has had to conform to the requirement of that thought and to respect its rhythm. It follows that this book on myths is a kind of myth.' It is hard to imagine the full consequences of such a total submission to the imitative fallacy. Certainly one feature is the selectivity which proceeds from the imagination's control. Suppose a far vaster work than *Mythologiques*, a Lévi-Straussian compilation of the myths of the world, however much more detailed and exhaustive, it would still only isolate a chosen series of configurations, of myths in a localized rather than universal sense – of materials that have a shape because they were selected.

Of course such a selectivity or imaginative control fills perfectly the prescription of Robbe-Grillet of 'playing' with the component elements. And Barthes in a similar vein holds that the best defence against myth – in his derogatory sense

– is to produce an artificial myth, 'and this reconstituted myth will be a true mythology'. Perhaps it does not matter whether this sense of the capacity to 'play' need necessarily involve one with the higher arts. Yet in so far as play is not random invention, a fringe activity of *homo ludens*, and involves any relational element whatsoever, it implies the creation of some kind of form, however antithetical in spirit to the elements on which it may have drawn. The notion of 'language game' implies the notion of 'rules'. Although perhaps 'language' itself with all of the attached structural implications would make play with words more subject to rules, however redevised or arbitrarily employed, than the 'plasmatic assortment' possible say to the visual arts, where the freedom implicit in, at its crudest level, *montage*, is perhaps greater. Of course for Robbe-Grillet, in so far as the prescription relates to his own art, there is the transformation of a world of images into a world of language, from the flow of objects before the eye to the controlled situation in which there are 'rules of the game'. 'True mythology' is arrangement.

3 *The dying myth*

The pattern of substitution which was observed in the last section clearly indicates both a movement from larger to smaller in the scope which any myth may have, and from stronger to weaker in the fashion in which it is held. And the obvious death of so many global myths, exciting the anguish of writers from, say Arnold, to a very recent example like Chiaromonte, raised two interesting questions; how do such great myths die and come to be replaced by lesser? And why do some die rather than others? These are enormous questions and can only be considered briefly, largely to preface the question of how the literary trans-formations of myths in some way alter their characters and life-cycles. Also there is the further question of the mortality rate to which those very transformations are subject.

Kermode says 'fictions lose their power when they lose their explanatory force' and we have looked at the ambiguities that 'explanatory' involves. What is it to cease to find something explanatory? Victorian literature is rich in dramatic examples of the loss of faith, of the registering of the moment when explanations fail, and of the full range of consequences of such a failure. And we are well accustomed to those who made the painful transition from the Christian faith as a literal frame of reference to the same faith as an ennobling vision of mankind. There is a sense in which Kermode's remark puts him on the edge of conjoining fiction and unspecified forms of explanation. Yet the way is clearly open to a somewhat different sense of fiction: to take the example of a novel that wrestles all too directly with the problem of belief, *Anna Karenina*. The double sense of fiction is omnipresent in the relation of those hypotheses which Levin proposes, doubts, etc. and the fictional frame which surrounds them.

What is of course obvious is the vulnerability of the global myth when confronted by logical or empirical enquiry. The total view of whatever organized kind is undone by its totality, and its disappearance may be dramatic when confronted by either argument or unassimilable matter of fact. This again however is something one can regard as culturally conditioned. There have been moments in time when only the global sense would satisfy. Yet what is clear in modern society is its power to cleave to the fragment while silently discarding the whole. And the conditions that govern either satisfaction may be roughly shown: faith in a total scheme of things or faith in the multiple fragments of which one's world is composed are both totally different in their implications yet in a wide variety of situations interchangeable. From total explanation to fragmentary fixed poles is a more familiar path than the reverse, and a standard feature of the intellectual history of the last century.

I have tried to define the rôle of myth in this process in terms of its ambiguity, in terms of the imaginative parenthesis in which it holds the more precise commitment of other forms of belief, and in terms of the power implicit in it of shifting the levels at which one's sense of self and situation are possible.

Of course it is not only the great myths that die, and in using the term in the wide sense when so much of that use accepts the abandonment of explanatory power of a literal kind, we may pick up, try out, discard, revalue any of the multiple fragments to be found in the market-place. Myth's power over the imagination may involve the whole self or less and in such a variety of ways and degrees. One is perhaps too easily tempted to take the global myths as models, especially in view of the cultural importance of the dying of religious belief. But even that involves so much beyond the explanatory power, and when belief is gone and the images remain there is a half-nostalgic commitment to what a thing has been, as one may be attached to the values of a vanished social order while realizing perfectly that it is no longer viable and that the conditions for making it so are impossible to reproduce. The modern concept of myth points to the blurring of the edges of this process, and when we say that one myth replaces another we are accepting the gradual process by which convictions and attitudes alter. We also accept the degree to which such a process may be partial, self-deluding, or involve conscious adaptation or duplicity. De Tocqueville puts this in the context of changes in public opinion:

Time, events, or the unaided individual action of the mind will sometimes undermine or destroy an opinion, without any outward sign of the change. It has not been openly assailed, no conspiracy has been formed to make war on it, but its followers one by one noiselessly secede; day by day a few of them abandon it, until at last it is only professed by a minority. In this state it will still continue to prevail. As its enemies remain mute or only interchange their thoughts by stealth, they are themselves unaware for a long period that a great revolution has actually been effected; and in this state of uncertainty they take no steps; they observe one another and are silent. The majority have ceased to believe what they believed before, but they still affect to believe, and this empty phantom of public opinion is strong enough to chill innovators and to keep them silent and at a respectful distance.

Here the concept of 'opinion' is as loose as that of 'myth' and the nature of the 'great revolution' could be multiple in kind and degree. Both terms attach themselves to that area of attitudes and feelings where our vocabulary is most insecure. And this may be as in the death of love, where its power slowly and invisibly withdraws until the strange discovery occurs that what one has taken for substance is shadow.

But whether those attitudes are held as beliefs, opinions, myths, affections or even fashions, we feel the fever of the market-place, where the competition and openness to change make for a perpetual but evenly applied mortality rate. However far from the field of explanatory force, the incalculable pressures have created for us the kind of flux in which multiple substitutions mean endless forms of reciprocal danger and loss. A study of this would require understanding not of how particular myths die, or even how particular categories die, but of how all of the multiple levels imply the mortality of each other. If small myths are made out of the sherds of great ones, the precious remnants may become – as in a collector's world – passionately held, admired, honoured; or discarded, traded, or merely forgotten, like the decaying butterflies or dusty mineral specimens in Victorian country houses, fragments of some treasured aspect of life that has quietly slipped from view, their rôle in the psychic market-place less abandoned than forgotten.

I have claimed that the life of myth in its modern sense depends on the death of traditional myths, and feeds off them at another level. Two features of this have been described: the distancing involved in the overt fictionalization, and the pattern of substitution by which one sort of myth can work for another. However there is an important sense in which a reciprocal development takes place in which these two, the fiction in its own right and the fiction distanced in the context of a further arrangement, are responding to the same pressures and perform the same function. At this point, where literal explanation has been discarded, these two senses of fiction are fused. The 'mythicized' objects, attitudes, fragments of beliefs and opinions, and our 'arrangements' of them surround us in an uneasy continuum where the interplay is conditioned by our inner uncertainties and the *perpetuum mobile* of the market-place.

So Kermode is mistaken; it is in abandoning their explanatory force that our fictions retain their life, both in the imaginatively intensified fragment and the multiple rearrangement, which in works of literature play exactly upon the multiplicity of possible fictions, each an aspect of a world capable of at least some degrees of accommodation with itself.

But return to Stavrogin's dream. In what sense may such a dream lie or lose its power? Having abandoned everything of the Golden Age except the image in which it is grasped, does its very life depend on the suggestive power of the visual alone? This would hardly do justice to the imaginative dimensions we have already seen in Stavrogin's response. Yet can one also imagine a race of men for whom the image would be meaningless, for whom 'the sylvan paradise . . . without which nations cannot live' had lost its evocative power, and had deteriorated into the meaningless anecdote or unrelated image? Or can we imagine a kind of evolution in taste where the pure symmetries suggested by magic rings supplant the complexities of *King Lear* or *Anna Karenina*? Of course we can, although the *Hamlet* anecdote may suggest certain transformations in a form of 'life'. But there is also the sense in which the distancing of the dream is its salvation.

Suppose the sylvan paradise or the conflict of Lear with his daughters should in another age seem the one silly and the other comic. The shift of our normative sense of what causes anguish or pain might make the great tragedies hilarious, or comic ploys unintelligible. There are certainly societies sufficiently alien to our own in which reactions might violate any sense that we have of the decent, humane or appropriate. And if the evolution of mankind should follow such a course we might see in it a mixture of the possible and inexplicable. Only our frail confidence that the important values of one's culture somehow survive transmission might seem the required qualification – along, perhaps, with the suggestion that whatever necessary stories such alien sensibilities developed would in turn have their frame of reference and require their interpreters.

4 An analogy

It has been clear that this is not a book about myth, but rather the analysis of a related group of modern pre-occupations, for which the concept of myth has been re-invented

– multiply re-invented, not in itself as a substance, but as a matrix of transformations, standing not for a single *thing* but for a series of related possibilities. So for us myth is an inheritance and an invention, an escape and an obligation, a choice and a fatality, an indication and a denial. We have found in it what we have sought, after our fashion, and in whatever vocabulary happens to be our own made demands on something we have called 'myth', requiring it to answer in kind. This has left us without a theory of myth, because there is simply no ground on which 'theory' in a normally intelligible sense might possibly work. If sometimes we have seen patterns that might support a Lévi-Straussian analysis, we can see that their ground is contingent and the material subject to an eclecticism in interpretation that would render multiple forms of pattern possible. And even such a theory as this would only go part of the way towards accounting for the rôles of the notion of myth in literary thought.

The most constant feature of the use of 'myth' has seemed the conjoining of two elements: an imaginative unity which has some recognizable formal properties, however much they may violate our conventional notions of literary form, and which still provides a form of imaginative escape from the world of logical implication or practical consequence. If such a duality describes the function of myth for the literary mind, does it also describe anything of the rôle of literature for our culture as a whole? Or do we see in such capacious functions rather an identity of demand as to what literature has asked of myth and culture has asked of literature? One thing I think we have seen we cannot do, considering the emptiness of myth as a conceptual catch-all, is convert those moments when the concept seems a necessary part of our thinking into an overarching explanation containing such moments. What would be necessary in such a case would be a grandiose psychology of myth, figuring forth the underlying causality of this order of demand and relating it to whatever monomyth seemed appropriate to the crisis discerned in our civilization, creating a speculative formula linking situation, psychological account and mythical form. Enough reasons have been given to show the mixture of futility and headiness in such an impressionistic enterprise.

Similarly, neither can the moment of insight carried in the inventive adaptability of 'myth', a notion created for us at least as the vehicle of imaginative flexibility, catching the unimagined conjunction or fresh angle of vision, become the basis of a method. We have seen already that Eliot's evocation of a 'mythical method' is little more than a figure of speech. And we have seen the use of such a method in interpretation in the rather pedestrian practitioners of myth criticism.

Of course a word may demand that we consider the meeting points of its multiple sense and contexts. But to do so is to do violence to a presupposition of unity. The 'mythical method' in literature as Eliot may have understood it, the critical procedures devised by myth critics, the mythical substratum in which Jungians see an underlying identity through multiple forms, or the 'logic' of myth as conceived by Lévi-Strauss, may seem at first glance to have more to do with each other than they do at a further look, and the excitement we derive from any conjoining of these distantly related spheres is often that of the meretricious joy of misunderstood context.

Further, the level of expectation is so different in those particular contexts to which particular disciplines are attached. If the study of myth is in some circumstances a scholarly or even structural analysis undertaken with respect to a large number of primitive tales, it may be yet another part of the dog-food of knowledge, to be chewed out by the appropriate professionals and judged in that more precisely calculated relation to the appropriate techniques and cultures which are necessary in the case. If on the other hand it is the projection of literary and quasi-religious mythomanes, the explorers of psychic dimensions for whom myth is a key to hidden forms of knowledge, the understanding of individual myths reflects the special pleading of the angle from which the myth is seen – often marked by a large degree of the inaccessibility which its special character bestows from the larger, more diverse and indeterminate body which we have come to call myth, creating that kind of specialization which effectively removes 'myth' from the world of common discourse. Finally, if it is a study of certain forms of the imagination – as I have largely treated it – it exists at a different level of generality from the others, and is too largely conceived as a vehicle of the imagination's 'mercies' or intensifying powers, moving it slowly away from the more concrete features which others would attach to their image of myth. 'Mythopoesis' is one of those terms which seems to have a maximum of sag in its elastic.

Yet if our interest is often greatest in that expansive or suggestive power that the word 'myth' has conveyed in some sense of possible access to a newer and more penetrating understanding of ourselves, or if the peculiar magic of the word alone has seemed to underwrite a more lively sense of the situation to which it is applied, we are still constrained to reach from this to some context in which such a power can be situated, and to try to conjoin the open-ended with some acceptable form of rigour. Perhaps at least part of the excitement generated by Lévi-Strauss lies in the sense that he has moved from the professional frame of reference to being the sort of philosopher of the imagination whose 'science' seems less like our familiar and all too deflationary empirical ground than a series of dazzling conceptual 'essays' concerning the nature of man. And if regarded as such he perhaps emerges less as a scientist (as he seems to see himself), or philosopher (as some of his critics have claimed), but like his master Rousseau, as a man of letters, with all of the freedom and openness to the multiple claim that such an identity implies, where the creative move seems to violate what are accepted as the normal canons of scientific method, and the most highly elaborated 'logical' rigour working through the metaphor of musical structures hints at laws of the imagination of the most consequential but elusive kind.

Of course, when critics assume that Lévi-Strauss has discovered a 'logic' of myth, the word 'logic' itself, like Eliot's 'method' is used figuratively. For if logic in its normal sense involves implication, the 'logic' of myth suggests simply the persistence of fundamental patterns which are subject to a series of formal permutations. These may or may not correspond to actual transformations which myths undergo, but the many forms of repeated symmetries and asymmetries, of similarity and difference and opposition, suggest a 'system' in which all of the parts are intelligible in terms of each other. Yet the relationships of mythical variants seem more an interesting form of contingent fact than a logic, and the connectives more a matter of discerning the figure in the carpet than the designation of a 'system'. Even if from any one pattern we can derive the permutations, they are of course not predictive, but simply an exercise in intellectual design. And part of the charm of the transformation 'system' is that of the unexpected, the suddenness of a change in direction, the incredible and unpredictable detail which leads to a wholly asymmetrical transformation, and which is as much a part of the 'logic' of the closed order as anything else.

And as system it would seem to have the sort of unity that functions like the unity of literary works themselves: the 'completeness' being of an imaginative order. And in so far as the system itself has a totality of function, as an order of internal relations in its confrontation with the random or contingent or the flux of time, the Proustian analogy given by Lévi-Strauss himself suggests a homology of function. The parallel lies on two levels: those which we have seen in many forms in the working of internal structures where a powerful design governs the workings of beginnings and middles and ends, or of a working out of fate's own dispositions in patterns which read the quasi-universalizability suggested in myth, where the echoes move beyond the particularity of the literary occasion. But in the closing pages of *L'Homme nu* the Proustian comparison helps to evoke the further level, where the relational order within the body of myth re-enacts the artist's ordering in the ultimate human confrontation with time.

So suppose a system, which in its character of the self-contained confronts the sequential order of historical change with the eternal reservoir of myths, which defies entropy through its perpetual metamorphoses. The discoverer of a figurative logic has juxtaposed another imaginative world to that of process: the model of the world of myth, however richly figured in its structural features, however ingenious the discovered homologues, projects through those very structural features the outlines of a sublime fiction. Less formally pure than its musical analogues, less entangled in the matter-of-fact and connotative morass than the great novelists, its internal play of difference within symmetry may also express beyond its immense variety a further symmetry of intent. The step is beyond history into structure, beyond the randomness of things into an order whose turbulent fragments are never stilled, yet which nevertheless enables us to envisage the totality which contains the movement, which in setting us beyond history sets us beyond time.

It is not of course that time can be stopped, but as in the Proust passage that Lévi-Strauss quotes 'the moment's freedom from the order of time, has re-created in us, in order to feel it, a mankind released from the order of time'. And history the destroyer may so be imaginatively contained, as the gesticulating zombies of the matinée of the Princesse de Guermantes may in memory be recaptured, who through the novelist's powers are re-linked to their former selves, given their place in the great novel which places them beyond time's hand. May the social scientist rectify time's injustice where the artist has not? There is no reason to think so from the homology of both structure and intention. And the 'triumph of structure' may seem to us for all of its undoubted richness of observation and analysis like a scientific mythographer's version of Stavrogin's dream, appealing in its visionary power, and yet in its beauty alien to us and our situation, its model 'demonstrations' preserving their ambiguity, explaining within their own terms what can never step beyond them. The ambiguous satisfactions seem aesthetic and detached.

We should perhaps not forget that the sensibility which called, not only for 'a myth' but 'myth' may also take flight from it, and the decline of myth criticism may have shown us less that the limitations of a method have been measured than that a certain form of magic has ceased to beguile. For us the self-contained kingdom, the dubious deductions, are less relevant than that ordering which has a more immediate and less elaborate rôle. Less part of a grand construction than a moment of imaginative intensity, less of an evolved choice than a derived fatality, a frail and momentary demonstration capable of shaping within the historical flux – if through its own shape pointing beyond it – some passing identity useful to mankind, even when the more transcendent of mythical claims seem 'to mask the lack of power which has deserted us of bringing reality to the new' and to concentrate as did Arnold long ago, with a fierce stubbornness upon the primacy in all our experience of the 'contingent cause – the death of the Gods'.

Further reading

The bibliography of myth is enormous, and even more varied than the present text suggests, much of it in areas which I have not touched such as prehistory or folklore. So I shall hardly do more than point to other bibliographies in which a fuller range of material may be found. Nor does it seem useful to give a full account of my own sources: I have used so much that is not referred to in the text, and much of what is referred to is merely by way of example. What follows is simply to indicate those works which will enable a reader to follow up the main lines of my argument. Except for the anthologies mentioned at the beginning, references follow roughly the order of appearance in the text, or of relevance if no reference appears. I have mentioned only one of the often multiple editions in which many of the works cited have appeared, usually choosing on the ground of convenience, although that is not always easy to determine.

Four anthologies offer a wide range of reading: *Myth and Literature: Contemporary Theory and Practice*, edited by John B. Vickery, University of Nebraska Press, 1966; *Myth, a Symposium*, edited by T. A. Sebeok, Indiana University Press, 1958; *Myth and Mythmaking*, edited by Henry A. Murray, Beacon Press, Boston, 1968; and *Mythology*, edited by Pierre Maranda, Penguin, Harmondsworth, 1972. Vickery has an extensive bibliography, specifically concerned with the convergence points of myth and literature, but is rather weak on European works. It might be supplemented by that of Maranda, more recent, more distinctly anthropological and directed towards contemporary European structuralism. A general work on myth to which I have referred also gives useful references: G. S. Kirk, *Myth: Meaning and Functions*, Cambridge University Press, 1970.

Chapter 1

For his translation of 'Stavrogin's Dream (in his *Dostoevsky: Essays and Perspectives*, Chatto & Windus, London, 1970) and helpful discussion on Dostoevsky's use of it, I am grateful to Professor Robert Lord. For Plato on myth see J. A. Stewart, *The Myths of Plato*, London, 1905 and Perceval Frutiger, *Les Mythes de Platon, essai philosophique et littéraire*, Paris, 1930. Roland Barthes, *Mythologies*, Seuil, Paris, 1957, has been published in translation by Cape, London, 1972. (The rather free translations employed in the text are my own.)

Discussion of the functional character of myth is to be found *passim* in the literature of anthropology, but see particularly B. Malinowski, *Science, Magic and Religion*, Anchor Books, New York, 1954; and A. R. Radcliffe Brown, *Structure and Function in Primitive Society*, London, 1952, and *Method in Social Anthropology*, University of Chicago Press, 1958. Freud's views on myth are scattered through his works, and unfortunately those with a more specific myth content such as *Totem and Taboo* do not fully represent them. Jung has explained the growth of his interest in myth in his autobiography *Memories, Dreams, Reflections*, Collins and Routledge & Kegan Paul, London, 1963. References to the subject abound throughout his work, with extended discussion especially in *Archetypes of the Collective Unconscious* and *Symbols of Transformation*, both in the Bollingen edition of the collected works, published in England by Routledge & Kegan Paul. See also *Essays on a Science of Mythology*, written with Karl Kerenyi, Routledge & Kegan Paul, London, 1957. For a Jungian view of Greek myth see Kerenyi's *The Gods of the Greeks*, Thames & Hudson, London, 1951. Works on symbolic transformations in myth often have Jungian affinities even if not a direct derivation. I have drawn on Joseph Campbell's *The Hero with a Thousand Faces* and *The Masks of God*, both in the Bollingen Series, both 1968. Also the studies of Eastern myth by Heinrich Zimmer, *Myths and Symbols in Indian Art and Civilization*, Bollingen Series 1947, and *The King and the Corpse*, again the Bollingen Series,

1948. A cultural historian of myth who is concerned with the repeated patterns and transformations of myth is Mircea Eliade, especially *The Myth of the Eternal Return*, Bollingen Series, 1954, and *Myth and Reality*, George Allen & Unwin, London, 1964.

The great four volume work of Lévi-Strauss on myth, *Mythologiques*, Plon, Paris, 1964–71, is in the course of translation. For those who are not anthropologists the 'overture' to *The Raw and The Cooked* and the concluding section of *L'Homme nu* offer some more general reflections, and one should in any case begin with the essay 'The Structural Study of Myth' from *Structural Anthropology*, Basic Books, New York, 1963. There is an excellent study of his method by various hands in *The Structural Study of Myth and Totemism*, edited by Edmund Leach, Tavistock, London, 1967. Leach also has written a very useful introduction to his work: *Lévi-Strauss*, Fontana, London, 1970. And see the issue of *Yale French Studies* on 'Structuralism', 1966. As structuralism is an approach or method applicable to other matters than myth, and is in any case not a term of explanation I have not included it in the text as a 'theory', nor do separate references to it seem useful here.

Ernst Cassirer's principal work on myth is the second volume of *The Philosophy of Symbolic Forms*, Yale University Press, 1955. Also, *Language and Myth*, Dover, New York, 1944.

For literary uses of myth there are many references in Vickery, but the larger number will be in the bibliographies of the particular writers in question. Eliot's review of *Ulysses*, 'Ulysses, Order and Myth' is from the *Dial*, lxxv, 1923; it has been reprinted in Ellmann and Feidelson, *The Modern Tradition*, Oxford University Press, New York, 1965. Richard Chase, *The Quest for Myth*, Louisiana State University Press, 1949. Ted Hughes's adaptation of Seneca's *Oedipus* is published by Faber & Faber, London, 1969. Paul West's effusion is called 'Adam's Alembic, or Imagination versus mc^2', and may be found in *New Literary History*, vol. 1, no. 3.

Chapter 2

Several of the examples of myth criticism have been taken from Vickery. For reasons which will be obvious from the text they have not been identified. Dorothy Van Ghent's essay 'Clarissa and Emma as Phèdre' is from the *Partisan Review* for 1950 and was reprinted in *The New Partisan Reader 1945–1953*, New York,

1953. Northrop Frye's systematic development of myth criticism is principally found in the famous *Anatomy of Criticism*, Princeton University Press, 1957. Some other examples have been taken from *A Natural Perspective*, Oxford University Press, New York, 1965. There is a good volume of critical studies in English Institute Essays, *Northrop Frye in Modern Criticism*, edited by Murray Kreiger, London, 1966, which contains a bibliography.

Chapter 3

Frank Kermode, *The Sense of an Ending*, Oxford University Press, New York, 1967. F. E. Sparshott, 'Notes on the Articulation of Time', *New Literary History*, vol. 1, no. 2. The story about Hamlet is from 'Miching Mallecho: that means witchcraft' by Laura Bohannan. Originally a Third Programme talk, it was published in *From the Third Programme*, Nonesuch Press, London, 1956. The remarks of Robbe-Grillet, adapted from an article in *Le Nouvel Observateur* for 26 June 1970, have been distributed with *Projet pour une révolution à New York*, Les Editions de Minuit, Paris, 1970. The epigraph is from a remark quoted in *Alain Robbe-Grillet* by André Gardies, Seghers, Paris, 1972. Nicola Chiaromonte, *The Paradox of History*, Weidenfeld & Nicolson, London, 1971.

Among the many works consulted, but for one reason or another not referred to in the text, of special interest to students of literature is *Mythe et épopée* by Georges Dumézil, Gallimard, Paris, 3 vols, 1968–74.

DATE DUE